Leadership Rules

To Mona, Katriona and Ingeborg

LEADERSHIP RULES

by

Michael Shea

CENTURY
LONDON SYDNEY AUCKLAND JOHANNESBURG

Published in Great Britain in 1990 by Century
An imprint of Random Century Ltd
20 Vauxhall Bridge Road, London SW1V 2SA

Century Hutchinson Australia (Pty) Ltd
20 Alfred Street, Milsons Point, Sydney, NSW 2061, Australia

Century Hutchinson New Zealand Ltd
PO Box 40-086, 32-34 View Road, Glenfield,
Auckland 10, New Zealand

Century Hutchinson South Africa (Pty) Ltd
PO Box 337, Bergvlei 2012, South Africa

Typeset in Sabon by SX Composing Ltd, Rayleigh, Essex

Printed and bound in Great Britain by
Clays Ltd, St Ives plc

British Library Cataloguing in Publication data

Shea, Michael, 1938 May 10 –
Leadership rules
1. Leadership
I. Title
303.34

ISBN 0 7126 3602 1

Contents

INTRODUCTION

'Nations would be terrified if they knew by what small men they were ruled.'

Charles-Maurice de Talleyrand

Most leaders do not lead. They do not even manage. They merely hold a title, and are figureheads at the head of the pack. In my experience, many up-front men and women are just that and no more: pseudo-leaders, marionettes, chairmen of committees of equals at best. Their leadership is a façade; there is little of substance behind the mask of authority.

Yet leaders of countries, of movements or of industrial companies are frequently vested in the public mind with superhuman qualities. They become the stuff of legends. In practice they are often very ordinary men and women thrown to the top of the heap, victims rather than arbiters of history, carried along by events rather than determining them. They are pawns rather than players, adequate figures whose strings are pulled by an authority system or by a leadership team, that drives, guides and presents them: thus, for example, the eight years of Ronald Reagan's rubber-stamp Presidency.

Because of the positions I have held in the past, I have had the opportunity to meet a large number of presidents and premiers, national and international leaders of all sorts and conditions, as well as a wide cross-section of top people from industrial, commercial, academic and social life. Many of them, whatever their reputations, were very average people indeed.

More importantly, I have had the chance to meet, talk to, work with and observe working at close hand, their press secretaries, spokesmen, public relations staff, image-builders and speech-writers. Even minor leaders of small countries or organizations may run large teams of such people. I can remember, while I was at Buckingham Palace, receiving a long Foreign Office telegram listing what I believed was the foreign press corps that was arriving to cover a certain presidential state visit. The list of around a hundred turned out to be the presidential press office and its staff, coming in on a special VIP flight.

If I were asked to draw one conclusion at the beginning of this book it would be that image in leadership matters just as much as, if not more than, reality, and that the real qualities of a leader are often in inverse proportion to the number of image-makers on his or her staff.

Even strong leaders need some advice on presentation. Everyone does. But strong leaders speak for themselves. Weak leaders and weak organizations need to be dressed up in the clothes of authority and wisdom by the image-makers of life. In an age of mass communication, leaders are judged by their television and newspaper images, and these images are manipulated to hype action and cloak inaction. Leadership struggles, as with the one in Romania after the execution of the Ceaucescus, may now be carried out live on television. Power on that occasion meant not so much the battles in the streets, but keeping control of Studio 4 in Bucharest's television station. In Britain we have to make do with the relatively mild broadcast images that emerge from the House of Commons. But all the same, in the leadership rule book the leader who presents him or herself well wins. These are the majority, the window-dressed leaders of the world, who have been created by skilful packaging, public and press relations, and who, in the end, will be destroyed by the same process. To misquote de Gaulle, the graveyards are full of such men, once thought to be indispensable.

The ability and effectiveness of any leaders are only as strong as they are perceived to be by those who are led. No matter how many leadership qualities a person has, they are worthless if no one recognizes them. Hence the growing practice world-wide, and particularly in societies where the media has replaced parliaments as the forum for 'democratic' debate, of building up and managing the image and reputation of the would-be or incumbent figure of authority.

This is why one sees selection teams, be they in political parties or causes or sometimes even in industrial enterprises, go for the most stable people, and those who come across best on the media, rather than the most able. Image creation works for the individual; it also works for the organization which that individual is going to lead. Malcolm Muggeridge put it well when he said of Anthony Eden, 'they asked for a leader and were given a public relations officer'. I call these pseudo-leaders marionettes. Puppets manipulated by unseen hands pulling strings. The famous Salzburg marionettes even have mouths that open and shut and appear to speak their own thoughts. But the voices are those of the manipulators, speaking for them from behind the backdrop.

There is a current Americanism, 'the empty suit', used to describe executives who dress and present themselves well, who know the right company buzz-words, but who have negligible skills or management ability of their own – save one: they have got where they are by not putting their feet wrong. The Scots coined a similar sobriquet centuries ago – 'Toom Tabard', the empty tabard or sleeveless dress – to describe the English puppet or vassal king Balliol, put on the throne of Scotland by King Edward I.

Marionettes or empty suits appear constantly in high leadership positions: they are the titular vice-presidents of life. They got there because they had fewer enemies than their opponents. They got there by going with the prevailing wisdom. There were better candidates and more red blood around when Reagan or Foot or Alec Douglas Home were chosen. But the selection boards went for the lowest common denominator rather than the highest common factor.

Marionettes are legion in big organizations everywhere. They exist best in highly structured bureaucracies, where the real people run things from one level below the top in order to cope with such leadership. Small, lean units cannot allow themselves such luxuries. Marionettes excel where there is a great deal of built-in formality and a great many tiered committee procedures to stifle initiative and encourage uniformity. They float on the top, always working through the turgid hierarchy of decision-taking rather than around it. They are the non-Darwinian leaders, lightweight polystyrenes, merely filling a space. They are there when the bloodstained pack has finished fighting the leadership battle. They emerge clean-coated and trouble-free when everyone else is tired and fed up with the struggle.

Marionettes who do not rock the boat and do not speak out of turn rise to the top because they always do the right thing, never stepping out of line. The last thing they do is try to stimulate change, take risks, or inspire. But they are not necessarily incoherent: sometimes they are very glib indeed. They are the guardians of the *status quo*, stiflers of energy, keepers of rule books, opponents of pluralism. They are the safe candidates for leadership slots. They are chosen not because the selectors think they are best, but because they can be agreed upon.

I am not arguing that leadership is all perception and image and that most leaders are marionettes. You need only to look at the past to see that is not the case. Churchill and Macmillan and de Gaulle were very real, and all retained an aura of leadership even after they left office. But what of Carter or Wilson or Edward Heath? What happened to the public perception of their leadership qualities? Why do some leaders retain their reputation while others disappear into well-deserved obscurity? The answer is that while in reality there is an obvious distinction between real leaders and the marionettes, in practice the image-creators can blur the distinction, at least for a time.

Of course there are real leaders, sometimes great leaders, men and women who rise above mere title or appearance to drive and inspire and get things done. Some such leaders are almost inseparable from the nationalist spirit of their country. As with Napoleon or Wellington, so it was with Bismarck, the first Chancellor of the German Empire, whose life history was the history of Germany itself. Dictator as he was, there was no doubting his authority and skills which led to the creation of a unified German state. Yet even he was aware of the importance of reputation, knowing that false perception can, if unchecked, win out over even the strongest reality.

Setting aside for the moment the whole question of image creation, what do I mean by leadership? Every political, economic and social philosopher throughout history has had his or her definition of it and the qualities required for exercising it. Every contemporary handbook on 'How to get to the top', 'manage', 'thrive' or 'win' has its catalogue of leadership or management virtues. Most commentators do not even distinguish between leadership and management – two vastly different functions within any organization.

We have all come across good leaders who, because of lack of time or inclination or because they are mercurial by nature, are incapable of consistent management. Some good managers, on the other hand, have a few leadership qualities thrown in. Because it is so much to do with the relationship with those to be led, and is based on the will of the many, I am convinced that leadership depends on inherited character as well as on training and experience. Management is a skill which can be learned. Leadership, like successful politics, is a calling for which no amount of training is ever going to be enough. Some leadership qualities can be learned, but only if an extra something is there already.

For a leader is, above all, an agent of change, an inspirer and developer who shows the way forward. A leader must integrate people and ideas by drawing from past and present experience, to show how the future should be shaped. A leader has to bring both colleagues and followers along in a way that is at once pragmatic and meaningful, persuading them to share objectives in order to achieve what was considered impossible before.

But there is no point in having drive and vision without support. A good leader also knows enough of the subsidiary skills of management to ensure that goals, once formulated, are achieved in the most effective way. A good manager may be able to keep even an inefficient organization running relatively smoothly. But many people will have seen, as I have, that the arrival of one good leader can transform a demoralized organization, whether it be a nation, a regiment, a company, or a football team. Lee Iacocca, for example, single-handedly transformed the moribund Chrysler Corporation, while Lord King, backed by a first-class team, turned an ailing giant into the modern British Airways, 'the world's favourite airline'. On the world stage, the unique example of President Gorbachev has transformed not one nation but half the world. His problem is that while he can take the initiative and unlock the prison door, as de Klerk in South Africa can free Nelson Mandela, it is less certain that he can control the events that flow from that action.

Leadership has to be looked at in the context of the society in which it operates. What are the existing power, class and élite-group structures? Does the country, organization, political party or industrial company prefer one particular leadership type, chosen from a scale ranging from the despotic through to the consensual? How often is unitary, as opposed to group, leadership really possible in modern society, given the power clusters, the checks and balances and the underlying structure within any system of authority? Are leadership skills commonly applicable and therefore transferable to different branches of society? Walter Bagehot wrote that the summits of various kinds of businesses, like the tops of mountains, are much more alike than the parts below. So does a good general necessarily make a good president of a country or chairman of a cricket club?

In terms of enduring reforms of law, of government, of administration, of military organization, there are few who have left so much that has lasted as Napoleon, and few who have had such an effect on the structure and future of all Europe. But was he born with the qualities of leadership, or did he acquire them on the long march to the top; and how would he have functioned in a world at peace, rather than a world of war and bloodshed? While times of crisis and times of tranquillity require divergent attitudes, and while different groups in society – political, industrial, social – require different leadership skills, I am convinced that there are basic qualities that are common to all leaders or change-makers in every walk of life.

A flexible leader will also, without necessarily departing from his or her basic goals or principles, know how to adapt or cut their style according to their following or audience. Their self-presentation and wielding of authority will be adjusted to suit a board of directors, a cabal of shop stewards, or the cynicism of the media or the City. The mask will smile or scowl, but the reality will continue beneath.

Central to everything is reputation and an ability to communicate in the goldfish bowl of public life. Pseudo-leadership by marionettes, which is largely 'hype', may in fact become real before it is found out. At its simplest, this is because having or acquiring the right image – a reputation for leadership – is the key to leadership itself.

Chapter 1
Leaders: Born or Made?

THE POWER / LEADERSHIP RELATIONSHIP

'As usual, I have against me the bourgeoisie, the officers and the diplomatists, and for me only the people who take the metro.'
Charles de Gaulle

Setting aside for the moment the marionettes or pseudo-leaders, are real leaders born or made? The debate goes back to Plato and beyond. In real life many are doubtless born with the requisite qualities, but few try or are given the opportunity to develop them. Most of them, 'born to blush unseen' in Gray's words, are destined to remain

Some village-Hampden, that with dauntless breast
  The little tyrant of his fields withstood;
Some mute inglorious Milton here may rest,
  Some Cromwell guiltless of his country's blood.

Many do achieve greatness through their own

efforts, but even more have it thrust upon them. There is a sub-category whose strength lies in the conviction that the world needs them. As General de Gaulle modestly noted, 'It is my duty, once again, to impose national interest on the Nation.' He meant himself.

In the born or made battle there are two distinct camps, the *nature* group and the *nurture* group. They have long debated the role of the individual of substance in a changing world. Carlyle, Nietszche, Emerson and others argued the case for innate personal characteristics; in their view leaders possess qualities superior to those of their fellows, unique talents which enable them to take their pre-eminent place in the world of decision-taking. Leaders by this account possess charisma, that extraordinary quality which, coupled with other talents, allows them to play out their role. Military and naval history is particularly full of leaders who were obviously born with the requisite qualities. Washington, Wellington, Nelson, Montgomery and a host of others rose to the top not through preferment but simply because of their abilities, both strategic and personal, which enabled them to inspire their men, and most importantly, to win.

Or did they? Where would any one of them have been without a good war to allow them to show and prove their mettle? Would we remember them without their battle honours, their Trafalgars, their Waterloos, their Alameins? Thus the nurture groups, the proponents of *Zeitgeist*, argue by contrast that leaders are a reaction to the needs of the time and situation. They fill a role in society, whether in war or in peace. If one departs, another takes his or her place, some doing the job well and others badly.

In the modern world I believe that we have to blur this distinction. The qualities of leaders or potential leaders and the situations they face have to merge. Sometimes this works, sometimes it doesn't. A good war lord does not necessarily become a peace-maker, not an effective crisis manager a good captain of industry, though the image-makers may argue differently.

Modern industrial leaders can still play at being ruthless nineteenth-century business tycoons, appearing to brook no opposition. But increasingly they have to compromise with the conventions and rules of contemporary business society, by going through the motions of following consensus leadership methods.

Whatever the relative merits of the nature or nurture schools, in most societies such considerations used not to affect the background from which the leadership cadre was drawn. In primitive tribes (and in royal Britain today) a dynastic system of replacing monarchs or chieftains prevails, to allow for an orderly transition at times of succession. Conflicts over who takes over from the boss are often messy affairs (as we may observe in modern industrial tribes) and can lead to too many good warriors being slain: a waste of scarce resources. Dynasties obviate this.

If not dynastic, then leaders were chosen from elite groups of families or classes to ensure the proper 'order' of things. In Britain, potential leaders in whatever field, from the Civil Service to banking to diplomacy, were chosen from the sons (and occasionally the daughters) of the elite, otherwise known as the Establishment – that matrix of official and social relationships within which power was, and often still is, exercised. It was essential, when you reached the podium, to be wearing not just the right cut of suit, but the correct school, college or regimental tie. You also had to have the right accent, on which there is more below.

There was once a virtually total correlation between leadership and class. The upper class ruled. You could not even begin to run in any leadership stakes unless you were of the right birth, background and education. In Britain a few relics of this remain. The right pedigree still produces a remarkably high proportion of the leadership of the City, the Church of England, the armed services and the Tory Party. The House of Commons today contains a sizeable number from all parties whose origins are firmly upper or upper middle class. But the vast majority of members of those classes are not leaders of anything in any real sense, whether social, financial or intellectual. It is far from inevitable that the well-born will progress to leadership, if only perhaps because they have been given life too easily. Those who succeed have usually had to struggle with and gain strength from adversity. It is this struggle which breeds the necessary determination to win.

Increasingly in modern times brilliant leaders rise from highly untraditional and unconventional backgrounds. A growing number come from relatively humble beginnings. In Victorian England the progress of a Jew, Benjamin Disraeli, to the post of prime minister was an astounding exception for the age. His success was largely a result of his style, his wide intelligence and his skill in debate. It was also due in part to the very special, almost romantic relationship he had with Queen Victoria. And she, like all dynastic leaders who inherit title through birth, was hedged around with conventions or constitutions which protect both monarch and people from the ups and downs resulting from their different abilities.

In any discussion about leadership, hereditary monarchies must fall into a category of their own, partly because they are hereditary and partly because nowadays (in Britain at least) they perform effectively and properly the duties that the state and constitution have prescribed for them. Good kings and queens follow bad ones, and vice versa, but in recent centuries, systems have been devised to limit the consequences of this, since their power is circumscribed by law and convention. Some leave their mark through force of character and longevity. Queen Victoria was an exceptional example of this, whose influence on the political and social life of Britain was profound (and, through the thoughtfully arranged marriages of her offspring, on that of most of Europe as well). Working through her ministers she ruled to a degree that none of her successors have been allowed to, with a sense of duty, wisdom and public service. Certain families have reigned if not ruled by tradition for decades or even centuries, such as the Medicis in Renaissance Florence and the Mountbatten Windsors in present day Britain. There are several other royal houses of great age, of which the heads tend to have merely titular or constitutional leadership roles.

But monarchs, be they absolute or constitutional, are the focus of strong emotional attachment. Without that they would not survive, since they lack the power or authority to remain in office without the backing of the executive and legislature of the state. Sentiment supports them as the focus of national loyalty. By contrast, political leaders, though they have been democratically elected and may be popular, are not often supported by sentiment as such, although in a constitutional monarchy like the British or Dutch, they try to gain it by having the monarch and head of state open Parliament, and thus appear to endorse policies to be carried out in his or her name. Commonly the head of state merely reads the words, and has no say in the decision-taking process. But is it really so different in many republics with titular leaders, or even some with executive ones? In Reagan's America I remember his advisers saying to him, 'Mr President, your thinking on

Nicaragua today is as follows . . .', or, 'Here is your speech. We have underlined the words we would like you to stress . . .'

Residual sentiment is not only to be found in royal lines of succession. Mahatma Gandhi, through his aesthetic example, his courage and his fasting 'to the death', made himself a leader/martyr for the case of Indian independence – and one of the greatest leaders of the century. After him, the Gandhi connection carried weight throughout republican India and Mrs Indira Gandhi, the daughter of Nehru, became one of the most effective women leaders of any age until her assassination in 1984. Her son Rajiv has yet to succeed to the same mantle of greatness.

All societies, not just developed ones, have their elites and always have had. Ask any social anthropologist about the status parameters of primitive, tribal or caste-dominated societies. Indeed ask any zoologist about the leadership of herds or packs of wild animals, the Darwinian triumph and survival of the strongest and the fittest. Leaders in the human and animal kingdoms are those that are most alert; and they remain chiefs until they lose their strength through age or defeat in battle. This is leadership at its most basic, the 'despotism tempered by assassination' favoured by Lord Reith as being the best form of government of all.

Other elites, just as much as royal dynasties, closed societies or clubs and doctors, lawyers and other professions, exist by controlling access to their numbers.

They find ways to ensure that only fellows of their choosing are admitted, through birth or lineage, education, examination, or financial standing. Such groups are the supreme practitioners of the closed shop. They guard their membership lists with every custom and convention they can muster. And because they are a self-elected elite, and can set the very rules by which they exist, they succeed in protecting themselves for long periods of time. After political or social revolutions history has shown that elites tend to regroup, reformulate the rules of membership, move the goal posts and start all over again. On the sidelines, of course, there are always many members of the elite who are not clambering over or clamouring at the gates of further privilege. They may not wish to join in, preferring merely to observe, to be entertained by or read about the leadership struggles of others in the columns of their newspapers.

'Class' and 'élite' are unfashionable words, but the fact is that top socio-economic groups, however defined, still do produce most of the leadership cadre in Britain today. The selection of 'people like us' by their peer group, resulting in a meritocracy of the rich and the well-born, is a constant and strong factor in Britain today. That is not to say that the membership of top groups remains consistent. There is constant change, as some people climb up while others drop out at the bottom. Of the chairmen of the top twenty UK companies, for example, less than a quarter went to university or public school; these are a new elite whose offspring will, if they wish, benefit from that elitism.

Society at large – business and political and social – for all its would-be egalitarian concerns, still has to recognize the truth underlying the late Lord Mancroft's remark: 'We are all born equal but some of us manage to get over it.' To put it another way, whether we start off on the same footing or not, we all end up either leading or being led.

LEADERSHIP AND POWER

'The Mandate of Heaven, that right to rule which the old Chinese recognised as conferring legitimacy on a government, was based on the simple proposition that if one contestant proved stronger than the other, the Mandate had passed to the victor. The Chinese are a very practical people.'

C. P. Fitzgerald

As I write, I read in *The Times* that George Bush and Mikhail Gorbachev are the two most powerful men in the world. Assuming that they have survived until you read this, what exactly does this 'power' word mean? Bernard Shaw called it 'the ability to achieve intended effect'; in modern times few individuals really have it in an unfettered form, and not least of these are Bush and Gorbachev. Absolute power is shackled by all sorts of constraints: the so-called powerful may be able to buy obedience, but, by and large, they are really only at the top of the heap that is the decision-taking process in any democracy, or budding democracy like the Soviet Union.

Not surprisingly, titles and positions are often confused with power. The trappings of power, or the stage on which leadership is displayed, are often of considerable importance to – if not the mainstay of – the authority and standing of a leader. Pomp and circumstance and ceremonial play a major role, as do the courtiers and acolytes in the antechambers of power. The crowns, the robes, the court dress, the startling tunics of equerries or bodyguards such as the Pope's Swiss Guard, even the pin-striped secretaries, the security guards in their dark glasses and the advisers who surround a president – all these combine to inspire awe and reverence, or acquiescence and dread. This is the appearance of power: but is it power itself?

Power has always been a major subject of study for political and social scientists, widely recognized, but difficult to comprehend or define. In my opinion pure power is a hypothetical concept in the real world, since it is usually hedged around with so many political constraints. Princes, presidents and premiers may, according to the headline writers, have 'decided' this or 'ordered' that; in reality they may be the driving force, but they can only wield authority when the constraints and qualifications of life have been met.

In the past, the leadership/power relationship was absolute. Thus in Eisenstein's film *Ivan the Terrible* Ivan asserts, 'You cannot lead, you cannot rule, without the menace of power.' His personal power was backed by a secret police and the rule of torture; it was all-embracing, and set the pattern for future Tsars of Russia. With the exception of the diminishing number of dictatorships of both right and left that still dot the globe, the leadership/absolute power connection disappeared with Hitler and Stalin. Certainly the 'menace' of power has been retained by some despotic political and industrial leaders of the 'fail to do this and that will happen to you' school, whose motto is *oderint, dum metuant* – 'let them hate me so long as they fear me'. The problem with such despotism, as the last Shah of Iran discovered, is that once you take the lid off the pot and allow some freedom to a long-subdued people, that pot will rapidly boil over with consequences that may be impossible to contain. Equally, when powerful industrial leaders take their hand off the helm or fade away their empires crumble too.

Power, even in chains, has one thing in common with leadership: both are not so much a *possession* belonging to the holder of an office, but a *relationship* with those who are led. Power suggests sanction, the ability to coerce or buy what is wanted. Modern leadership is more to do with inspiration or influence, manipulating people and getting them to follow you, making your goals and theirs the same. Good leadership is to do with personal bonding skills; bad leadership introduces the heavy hand of sanction. Relationships between the leader and the led should be a voluntary one, based on mutual perceptions of personal qualities and resources.

Looked at another way, leadership can be thought of as a mechanism of barter between the chief and the indians, a contract between them aimed at working out a system to achieve better common goals. Many leaders naturally come to believe in, or delude themselves into believing, such neo-Confucian theories of society: that for a society to prosper there must be a mixture of respect for authority and of bond loyalty and obedience between subject and ruler. A true leader is consequently seen as someone who can inspire the people, paving the way for all to reach a higher upland of expectations. In the process, leaders should promote not only themselves but, if they are wise, a new generation of future leaders who will advance on the same track.

All this has come to the fore whenever I have questioned today's leaders about what they see as their role. They tend to talk about qualities which they have found useful in themselves and, therefore, ones they think will be useful in others. Clone-seeking attributes abound. Among the most common are:

1 Wide practical experience – especially having worked outside their chosen field, to add to breadth of view. The best candidate will have lateral as well as vertical 'experience', as defined by Hegel: 'Experience has to run counter to expecta-

tion in order to call it experience.'

2 Numeracy/literacy.

3 Presentational and communication skills.

4 Self-assuredness (*not* assertiveness) or what pro-
moters of political charm schools would call *poise*.

Above all, modern leaders argue that the right relationship must be one based on trust – a largely voluntary arrangement. They also tend to say things like,
'I've no power. All I can do is encourage and motivate
people to do things. I can't force them.'

Admittedly, the way in which leaders think about
their own role usually tends to be camouflaged with an
element of quasi-modesty. They may talk as monarchs
used to, in the plural. 'We' manage the company or run
the country, rather than 'I'. They talk of 'our goals',
'our philosophy' and so on. They thereby further resist
the suggestion that they are all-powerful – at most they
claim they are first among equals, since anything more
suggests something almost pejorative, absolute, tyran-
nical. The leader, whether in the political or the industrial arena, wants to imply that decisions are taken
corporately, even if the facts are otherwise. They even
go through the motions of consulting and listening
before continuing to do their own thing: hence the dis-
parity between Margaret Thatcher's avowed commit-
ment to Cabinet decision-taking and collective responsibility and the autocratic manner in which she is said

actually to run things. Anything said by such leaders is intended to emphasize the voluntary and democratic nature of the relationship: thus 'we' in their terms, indicates not so much a royal arrogance but a *denial of ego*, a wish to identify or be at one with the nation, the company, Cabinet colleagues or whatever.

While the total leadership of any organization is seldom in the hands of a single person, in any effective operation there has to be one individual in charge, whatever these leaders say, in order to articulate and direct the strategy. My first and most important Leadership Rule is consequently very simple: *know them by what they do, not by what they are called*. The world is full of titles and ranks even in supposedly classless societies. In the leadership game, my first question is always: 'Who is *really* in charge?' My next question is, 'Does he or she initiate change?'

Chapter 2
The Functions of Leadership

'A U.S. President, above all, must be a leader, able to direct a large complex organization, or federation of organizations, and to deal with competing, often conflicting constituencies. A President must be a man of vision who knows in what direction he wants to guide the nation, a persuasive individual who can explain his means and ends in ways that will move people to support him.'

Time Magazine, 1976

The functions of leadership are self-evident, or are they? They obviously depend on the demands, requirements or potential of the office concerned. Some prime positions require very little of the holder in the way of skills or actions; others are extremely demanding in terms of the aptitudes and qualities required.

Leadership functions and leadership itself consequently rest on a combination of two pillars quite different from each other: the position held; and the stature and other attributes of whoever holds it. Thus: *Pillar I* is the office held by the leader of a country, government, party, company or other social group. It is their title, rank or position of legitimate authority:

president, king, premier, chairman, managing director, captain or whatever. *Pillar II* consists of the personal qualities, inherited or acquired, which enable the incumbent to do his or her job effectively. These may be great or minimal, depending on the requirements of Pillar I.

In some circumstances Pillar I will be a more important factor than Pillar II: where, for example, an accident of birth (as with inherited ranks) or mere time-serving brings eventual office. In most circumstances, however, the qualities that propel an individual to the top, summarized in Pillar II, are crucial.

Titles, ranks and other role designations can be beguiling. Ask any Establishment watcher. They imply the quality of leadership but do not necessarily invest the incumbent with it. 'Place' and status are essential to leadership, but the quality of leadership is more than mere position. We all know of political and industrial organizations which have nominal leaders but where all the real leadership decisions are taken below, before being merely rubber-stamped by the person whose name is at the top of the letterhead. Successive chairmen of the Tory Party, for example, have more often than not been relatively unknown and powerless figures in that part of the political establishment. Who had heard much of Peter Brook until he went to the Northern Ireland Office? The person who led the Tory Party between 1987 and 1989 was not him but, without a shadow of doubt, the Prime Minister. As I write the chairman of GEC is Lord Prior, who has a largely nominal role, while the man who is known to run it as managing director, as he has done for decades, is Lord Weinstock, and he alone. Some organizations appoint purely nominal chairmen as camouflage, particularly if they have a well-known inherited title. Even great universities, which ought to know better, do so. In its most extreme form this can give rise to the puppet leaders of every variety who have peppered political history. As Pu-Yi, China's last emperor, was a puppet to the invading Japanese, so Vikdun Quisling, the Nazi leader of occupied Norway, was the servant of his German masters. Such 'leaders' are not just benign puppets, and Quisling's name is now synonymous with treachery. Some states do deliberately give the head of state minor responsibilities of an executive nature, and not just in the monarchies. Over the decades since the war Germany has had several presidents whose names are largely unremembered or unknown outside the country. It is the chancellors – Adenauer, Brandt, Kohl and others who speak for their country in world affairs.

Vance Packard argued that the function of leadership was the art of getting others to want to do something you are convinced should be done. I tend to follow Mr Gladstone's view that the first essential for a good leader (he was thinking about prime ministers) was to be a good butcher. More seriously leadership is about:

1 *Initiating*: acting as a change-maker who gets things done.

2 *Articulating*: defining the strategy or the mission for the organization.

3 *Inspiring*: showing the way and getting others to follow through enthusiastic advocacy of that mission or cause; the inspiration of consensus.

4 *Monitoring*: measuring and being seen to measure results; fixing the standards to be followed and the goals to be achieved.

5 *Role-setting*: encouraging emulation by example; building trust through the creation of loyalty in both directions.

Leadership, as Napoleon said, is dealing in hope. It is about being able to initiate action and then to manage that initiative, about directing one's peers, and being both prepared for success and capable of handling failure. Leadership, whether generated by ambition or a desire to survive, is about leading from in front. Some leaders may have worked successfully from the back-rooms, but real leaders have to be perceived to have the towering height and presence of a Charles de Gaulle, whose clear and decisive eloquence and stubborn single-mindedness restored to a defeated France, and to the French, pride and a determination to take their place once again on the world stage.

A leader is consequently someone who knows clearly what his or her plan is and where they want to go, and who gets there with others following. They follow because he knows and they know that he knows, and because he has convinced them about what should be done and where their self-interest lies. He or she is someone who conserves whatever power or force they may have. They are leaders *because* they don't need to resort to force, who would say, with Sophocles, 'What you cannot enforce, do not command.'

Leaders build relationships in order to lead. But they also have to head organizations on a day-to-day basis, and the two do not necessarily go hand in hand. People and institutions may need different types of handling. To take a simple example: former President Reagan had a massive personal following yet was widely viewed as incompetent in his dealings with his administration. His advisers feuded with each other and with Mrs Reagan, not just over the great issues and policies of state but also over who was to be allowed the access necessary to handle him. And in a similar though humbler vein, the splendid, caring fatherly boss of a family company may lead it to bankruptcy. The strong leader, by contrast, will match relationships with people on the level of the individual with the handling of the larger task of running the organization as a whole. Management plus administration plus the L-factor — that is leadership. But what is the L-factor? What qualities and qualifications *are* required?

Chapter 3
The Qualities Required

'A true leader always keeps an element of surprise up his sleeve, which others cannot grasp but which keeps his public excited and breathless.'

Charles de Gaulle

'Strong beliefs win strong men, and then make them stronger.'
Walter Bagehot

De Gaulle followed his own advice and always kept France, and much of Europe for that matter, excited and breathless, though not always in the most positive of ways. He was a giant of a man both in presence and in personality. Keeping people guessing about what you are going to do next is a good way of holding their attention, and he did just that. The world's other politicians were left struggling to keep up. He was also a prime example of Bagehot's maxim: his belief in a strong France within a strong Europe did not endear him to the government of Britain at the time, but they could not ignore him because he refused to compromise – any more than he had done during the war, when Churchill complained that his 'heaviest cross was the cross of Lorraine'.

What is it that makes someone stand out as 'fit to govern' a country or to head an organization, company or team? Is Neil Kinnock 'fit to govern?' Is Margaret Thatcher? Was Nixon, Carter, or Wilson? What is this quality that political and economic commentators look for in candidates for preferment? Plato said that those who are too intelligent to go into politics are punished by being governed by those who are more stupid. Can we really say the same about industrial leaders? I doubt it.

What does always happen, I believe, is that in any leadership struggle *those who succeed usually do so because rival candidates lose.* The latter tend to do so by parading some inadequacy of personality, or policy, in front of the selectors or the electorate. That said, however, there are identifiable qualities which mark certain men and women out for the top. The Royal Military Academy at Sandhurst is said to have identified several hundred leadership skills. These tend to be of a precise man-handling and tactical variety. They stress qualities that build a discipline which will not break under fire, ones that are not often used or needed in peacetime. They include management tactics – how to keep the troops fit and fed and their boots dry in order to maintain high morale – which are essential to a regimented military system. They also include leadership concepts such as courage, physical fitness, in-itiative, integrity, loyalty, daring, team spirit, judgement, confidence and will-power. They are all basic disciplines of command which brook no argument and which have often proved their worth, not just on the battlefields of history. I approach leadership from a rather different viewpoint in listing the following ten principle qualities.

1 *Mission*

A clear, strong sense of mission; a focus; a bandwagon to leap on or a horse to ride. *Leaders need causes and causes need leaders.* It was Hitler, unfortunately, who said that the art of leadership consisted in concentrating the attention of the people against a single adversary; but many follow his general principle. An interest in winning, and not just in money or power, is essential.

2 *Flexible obstinacy*

Single-mindedness in pursuing that mission. 'First in war, first in peace, and first in the hearts of his fellow citizens,' George Washington, first president of the United States, was remarkable in his ability to meld warring factions together through the strength of his own personality. We have to beware, however, that such single-mindedness does not become tunnel vision, an inability to see beyond one limited objective.

3 *Opportunism*

A keen sense of timing and an eye for an opportunity; the ability to take decisions at the right time and act swiftly when required. This is sometimes best demonstrated by having a great short-term tactical ability. Many leaders are at most month-ahead thinkers. Some do well thinking only a few hours in advance. Leaders who 'think on their feet', the short-term operators, are the sprinters who may win out over their long distance rivals, even though each of their solutions is less than perfect. But short-term tactical opportunities must never be allowed to obscure the overall mission. It may be very appealing and momentarily satisfying to win a brief boardroom victory over a colleague or trounce an opponent, but the satisfaction will be short-lived if the skirmish has distracted you from the takeover battle that is about to break over you. In other words *short-term tactics must always serve the long-term strategy.*

4 *Self-assurance*

A belief in self – though not perhaps to the extent of Idi Amin, who declared, 'I am the most important person in the world.' He has more imitators than one would like to think, however, there being some value in a degree of immodest self-assurance. This is the gut-feeling factor: 'I feel it, therefore it's right.' It can display itself in a vivid independence, a lack of need to depend on others or simple pig-headedness. Hence history's epitaph on Field-Marshal Lord Montgomery's overweening self-confidence: his lack of any personal modesty and his idiosyncratic habits endeared him to the men of the Eighth Army just as they irritated those who only saw him from afar. An outstanding military leader with equally strong convictions, he remained a strangely isolated person, a loner in his private life – another mark of many great leaders, who find it difficult to relate well to others when there is no binding common cause or purpose.

5 *Substance*

A recognition that not only substance is required of a leader but also *a reputation* for being of substance. The strong element of image – the goldfish bowl effect – will be discussed later. Though a founder-leader of the new electronic age of mass communication, Lord Reith, legendary director-general of the BBC, was, through force of personality and great integrity and enthusiasm, a pre-eminent example of real substance as well as mere image.

6 *Endurance*

An ability to persevere, to survive, to endure. Leadership requires the ability to avoid the mistakes of history without being governed by fear of them. Generals are often accused of always wanting to fight the last war. The 1987 Stock Market crash had people studying the Wall Street collapse of 1929 to little avail. Case histories are useful but dangerous for leaders who would survive. The Polish trade union leader, Lech Walesa, endured. Despite all the setbacks, he moved doggedly from being a renegade trade union leader in the Gdansk shipyards, to being one of the cornerstones of the new movement towards political liberation in Eastern Europe; a man committed, against the odds, to seeing things through to a successful conclusion.

7 *Inspiration*
The intuitive spark, most important of all: the ability to light up others, to build an effective relationship with them, whether based on respect or on affection, or sometimes on fear of the consequences of not following. An inspirational military leader who is also perceived as a national hero at a time of danger is of great service to a country or a cause. The romantic fortitude of Admiral Nelson inspired not just his sailors but the whole of Britain. The manner of his death in his hour of victory only increased his lasting fame.

8 *Communication*
An ability to get the message across. Leaders

should also know how to listen and consult before they command. There is no doubt that *listening leaders last longer*. I will return to this subject later.

9 *Judgement*

And judgement embraces pragmatism. Simple men coming to leadership positions are often not as lacking in judgement as they like to pretend. Andrew Jackson, the seventh president of the United States, had a reputation for being a man of straightforward pragmatic views. Like Reagan he had a feel for the mood of the people, and it worked. Judgement means the ability to muster all the many influences, macro and micro, all the varied restraints and checks on leadership, and to come to the right conclusions. It also implies building up a good team to run the organization.

10 *Ambition*

On top of all the above, leaders need the *L-factor* to give them that extra push, that extra burst of energy to take them over the top. Kemal Ataturk's enormous personal drive, energy and dedication helped him to play his part in the founding of the modern state of Turkey. Ambition – national rather than personal – drove him to lead the Turks out of the medieval conditions in which they had been living.

There are many other qualities that contribute to the making of leaders or which bring out hidden qualities in them. Many people believe, for example, that challenges early in people's lives or careers or a taste for power acquired when young give rise to a future and continuing hunger for it. Bob Reid the new chairman of British Rail, is said to have been driven forward following a youthful accident when he lost an arm in his father's butcher's shop; and there are many examples of great industrial leaders like Lord Weinstock and Sir Peter Parker, who met early deprivation or hardship with the vow 'never again'. A number of others have had a strong guru in their past, a dedicated teacher for example (on the lines of the Jesuit boast, 'Give us a boy until he is seven years of age and we will have him for ever'), who has had a major effect on them. Which of us has not been inspired by some figure in our early lives, just as the South African thinker and writer Laurens van der Post is said to have had his effect on both the Prince of Wales and Margaret Thatcher.

Many outstanding business and industrial leaders especially have seized an early challenge or responsibility, or had it thrust upon them. At Hanson and other mould-breaking companies, managers are presented with such challenges very early on and are rewarded by substantial financial and other incentives if they are successful. The 'buggins'-turn' or dead men's shoes approach to advancement is a thing of the past. High fliers really can fly high and fast.

Another version of this is the *grit in the oyster factor*, the effects of struggle against adversity. President Franklin D. Roosevelt's battle against polio, was, according to his biographers, the grit in the oyster that inspired him to become a great leader in peace and war, and a particular champion of the underdog. And in a recent biography of Harold Macmillan it was argued that he was driven to succeed and pushed himself to the top as a result of discovering that his wife was having an affair with his parliamentary colleague Bob Boothby. This is a version of the 'adversity in youth' theory, which makes some people so determined to succeed. It is widely held, and there is much evidence for it among many of today's political and business leaders.

But of all these qualities it is undoubtedly the sense of mission that is paramount. Without it everything else falls apart. One can be driven and succeed through personal ambition, but to lead there must be a cause, a star to follow. This emerges most forcefully from any study of nationalism, that most inspiring and also most dangerous of political sentiments. At its best it is exemplified by people like Simón Bolivar, the liberator of South America from Spanish domination. The supreme patriot and hero in his own time, driven by a mission, had all the qualities of force and dedication necessary to achieve his principal aim. Similarly, Guiseppe Garibaldi, the Italian political and military standard-bearer, had one major cause which he carried throughout his life: the unification of Italy. Through his dashing bravery and his enthusiasm, he became a hero who captured the hearts and minds not only of his 'red shirt' followers, but of ordinary Italians of every persuasion.

Nationalism is an emotive cause in any society, but nowhere more so than in third world countries as they emerge from their colonial status. Leaders such as Jomo Kenyatta and Kwame Nkrumah in Africa or Mahatma Ghandi in India all grew with their mission, and each inspired his followers with a mixture of oratory and popular emotion. Each was also backed by the power derived from a knowledge of how the empire had been run, which stemmed from an education gained in the developed world in Moscow or London.

These are some of the attributes commonly found in and expected of leaders. Some are high-profile characteristics; others are low key, and form part of the personal make-up of the individuals themselves. But my main theme is that above almost everything else, leadership is to do with the perceptions of those who are led. So let me now dwell a little on that dangerous aspect of leadership: looking the part.

LOOKING THE PART

'The great leaders have always stage-managed their effects.'
Charles de Gaulle

All enterprises are to a greater or lesser degree known

by their leaders. The public at large personalizes governments, political parties and industrial companies, as they do theatre companies, football teams and so on. The leaders personify success or failure, whatever the democratic structure around them. It may be unfair and unjust, but it is how things are reported by the media. Companies are difficult to portray, to praise or vilify, even on the City pages. Not so their chairmen. Organizations know this, so looking the part becomes the key to many of the strategies to be pursued.

Presenting leaders to best advantage is an essential device rather than a devious one. Kings of old needed to look right in order to inspire. Edward I, for example, had a major advantage in that he was very tall for the age. Henry VIII was larger than life, both physically and in personality, thereby fulfilling his subjects' ideal for the perfect monarch. His fondness for women only enhanced his popularity and added to his charisma. He was the perfect man for his time, part tyrant, part the jovial 'bluff King Hal' of school history books. Today's potential leader, similarly, has got to look and sound right in front of the cameras and the crowds. Dress, voice, posture and style are all important.

Where these are lacking, for example where a leader is chosen by some inner group for reasons that ignore image (as with the Labour Party's choice of Michael Foot in 1980), it won't work. As with Edward I, even size and height have their place. Mrs Thatcher, speaking to an American audience, once said, 'Let our children grow tall, and some taller than others if they have it in them to do so.' The *Economist*, with its tongue not too firmly in its cheek, took this up and suggested that in industrial Britain, tall leaders such as Lord Hanson (6 feet 5 inches) and his partner Sir Gordon White (6 feet 6 inches) would always win out over the likes of Sir Michael Edwardes (5 feet 4 inches). But Napoleon was small, and so are many of today's leaders, so sheer size is not the only factor. Dignity or physical presence, if not size, are hard to beat when they run together with great drive and intellect.

How a leader talks is, like it or not, equally important – the so-called Pygmalion factor. Would Mrs Thatcher be where she is if she had not taken elocution lessons in received pronunciation? She is also said to have worked on two other factors: pitch and level of voice. However much we may deny that we are affected by someone's appearance or voice, all the polls reveal that accent matters as much as looks to a political electorate. We want our leaders to sound the part as well as be it. If they don't, they will find it much more difficult to climb up the ladder of success. Admittedly there are occasionally leaders who make a virtue of the blunt patterns of ordinary speech. Harold Wilson was not the only politician to have made great play of his man-of-the-people accent and style. But research shows that received pronunciation is equated by an electorate, and indeed by shareholders, with education and competence – both normally essential qualities for those seeking high office. Leaders have not just to know what they are about but must also, through what they say, be able to convince others that they know what they are about. There is no doubt that the ability to communicate, to speak on the public platform as well as round the boardroom table, is crucial: here image, the public visibility factor, matters more than substance. President Bush, for example, is not someone who can articulate well at times of triumph or tragedy, for instance when the Berlin Wall came down. His voice fails and his words, no matter how carefully drafted, collapse with it. With this example in front of us we see how presentation eclipses substance and turns it to nothing. Bush has yet to make a memorable speech. As someone remarked, so far, he is Gerald Ford without the pzazz.

Political parties in the democracies, if they are wise, consequently choose their leaders in terms of their ability to come across well to their members, the media, the electorate, and to a wider community, rather than for their purely political skills. Such leadership must be highly visible. This is much less true in industry and commerce, where leadership may still be largely invisible, exercised within the office and boardroom rather than on the public stage. But even here mood and practice are changing, and the captains of industry need increasingly to be able to communicate well with employees, shareholders, customers, the media and beyond. The leader's image is inextricably allied with the corporate image. In future companies which choose leaders who are poor communicators will be understood to be saying, in effect, that they don't feel the need to put their case in the best possible way, that their business record stands its own ground and needs no one to defend it. This is both foolish and dangerous, and they will rue the day when they find themselves in need of allies and support, or under threat of takeover from more visible and valuable predators.

A common downside of the ability to communicate well is a rather glib showmanship. All too frequently, and particularly in the political world, leaders are chosen more for their skill in convincing people, especially in a crisis, than for their attributes as captains of their particular management team, group or industry. They know how to 'smile nice, talk nice, sound genuine'. They have learned how to fake sincerity, while their words, actions, even policies, are largely dictated or at least formulated by those behind them. They can be carried by large organizations, but would destroy smaller ones which cannot afford such luxuries. Small businesses cannot carry passengers: everyone has a role to play and has to see it through. The car salesman in the local garage has to deliver as well as know the patter. Large organizations can, by contrast, argue that they need smooth talkers who are good at presenting even bad news to the outside world. I am not talking so much of the professional PR men and women who occasionally have a real job to do, but the 'protocol' people who are good on their feet and good at appearances, the oilers of reputation.

There is no doubt that the 'Welsh Wizard' Lloyd George's eloquence was a key factor in his reputation. This was particularly true during the First World War, when he inspired the nation if not his military commanders, with whom he had very mixed relations. He was also a skilled national negotiator, as emerged during the diplomatic meetings that culminated in the Treaty of Versailles. But his weakness and the cause of his eventual downfall was a lack of principle in his public and private life, and the resulting deep distrust of his friends and enemies alike.

The best leaders are an amalgam of both these qualities, who perform well on stage and also in the smoke-filled rooms where the real power-broking takes place.

A final attribute, not essential but very useful, is gravitas. A mysterious quality, it is a mixture of moral standing, experience, seriousness, weight, consequence, a reputation for getting things right, plus presence (I define presence as bearing plus dignity, voice, dress and looks). Gravitas can be expressed in both eloquence and by silence. The Japanese define it magically as 'the densities of the unspoken'.

These are some of the qualities required by a potential leader. How do they differ from those required by managers? The comparison is a useful one.

Chapter 4
Leaders and Managers

'To do great things is difficult, but to command great things is
more difficult.'

Friedrich Nietzsche

Managers are judged by their performance within set
parameters; leaders are judged by higher requirements.
They have a role that goes beyond management, administration or financial control. I have always believed
that good management requires some leadership qualities, just as leadership requires some management
qualities, for example over the choice of key personnel.
But in the main they are different functions in the running of any country, company or organization. Leadership is about change-making and the application of
that change. It requires extraordinary attributes and
ingredients that go beyond the efficient organization of
the *status quo*. But there is some overlap:

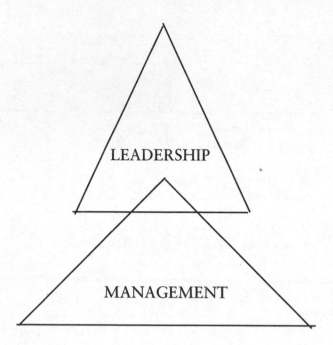

To be effective, leadership has to provide managers with the incentive to manage and to advance. In industry it sees above and beyond the corporate structure. I can hear the howls of anger when I suggest that management is relatively easy, while leadership is difficult. But they do require very different capabilities. Leaders don't always make good managers; good managers can't always become good leaders, though some go a long way towards it by imparting a wider vision to others. If one looks at some great historical leaders one can see the 'add-ons'.

Alfred the Great, for example, was a true leader in that he saw beyond the immediate problems and wars of his day. He spent a large part of his life planning the future prosperity of England, not only in founding a royal navy and other long-term measures, but also through creative administrative and management planning, and above all by developing an educational system that was centuries ahead of its time. In a later age Oliver Cromwell enacted administrative ordinances that were as fierce as any made by kings, which demonstrated his great management abilities on top of which came his leadership skills. In this century, by contrast, Benito Mussolini demonstrated the dangers of moving from management brilliance to political leadership. By all accounts he achieved major administrative reforms in pre-war Italy, but in the leadership stakes he was a mere puppet of Hitler, with a standing built on sand, as was demonstrated by the rapidity of his removal from power and his execution.

The qualities required for management and for leadership qualities and, more importantly, their different functions, can be summed up as follows:

LEADER	MANAGER
inspires	controls
thinks	does
motivates	organizes
initiates change	adjusts to change
challenges existing ways	accepts current practice
creates	administers
proacts	reacts
shapes actions	responds to circumstance
dictates	follows through
takes decisions	implements decisions

LEADER	MANAGER
sets objectives	gets results
sets the pace	concentrates on procedure
driving force	coordinator
unmethodical	methodical
front of camera	back stage
inspires loyalty	motivated by discipline
apart from others	involved with others
self sufficient	depends on organization

It is possible, of course, to dispute the placing of certain of these words in their respective columns, but the general trend in clear.

Leaders, overall, must have a breadth of long-term vision, and an ability to work the system that exists within the hierarchy below them. In the words of the commentator John Dodge, 'a leader of men must make decisions quickly; be independent; act and stand firm; be a fighter; speak openly, plainly, frankly; make defeats his lessons; co-operate; coordinate; use the best of any alliance or allies; walk with active faith toward danger or the unknown; create a staff; know, love and represent the best interests of his followers; be loyal, true, frank and faithful; reward loyalty; have a high, intelligent and worthy purpose and ideal.'

Management skills can be taught and they can be learned. Many huge institutions exist for that very purpose. Recently, however, I heard a major American industrialist shout, 'No more MBA's. I'm not employing any more MBA's.' Business schools are good if they train people to recognize that management is in no way a routine process. It is neither automatic nor robotic. No management problem is ever the same as the next one and anyone who tries to manage on the basis of a pre-set formula soon learns his lesson. The difference with leadership is rather like learning to play chess. The manager can easily learn the rules and the moves that each piece can make across the chequered board. The manager can learn to do this very efficiently and can beat mechanistic opponents. But in essence their function is methodical and subject to control: problem solving within well-defined limits. It takes leadership quality, the additional L-factor, to make a grand master, and even more so to realize that there are other games beyond the limits of the chess board.

Of course management is never just about the administration of the *status quo*, but is also concerned with plans for future change and with motivating a workforce to meet these plans and measuring the results. Leadership, backed up by management, provides the inspiration for moving away from old habits and processes, acting and controlling rather than being a victim of circumstance. Above all, leadership is flexible; management all too often is not allowed to be, and can motivate only on set and prescribed lines.

Leadership requirements are very similar in many different fields of endeavour. That is not to argue that a successful political leader would always make a good university chancellor, or that every great general, who has learned to rely on the military discipline of those under him, would make an equally good captain of industry. But there are many exceptions. General Sir Brian Robertson, the distinguished Second World War soldier, moved on easily and successfully to become head of Britain's Transport Commission when he retired from the army. Another military man, General Sir John Hackett, moved from being Commander-in-Chief of the British Army of the Rhine to become the very popular principal of King's College London in 1968.

Given the necessary background and experience, the skills in dealing with people and the required charisma, the sense of self and the sense of mission required of a leader are very similar across the board. The same cannot be said about management skills, which tend to fit more closely to specific job requirements. In practice, therefore, people who have been good in a top leadership position in one walk of life move across more easily to another. The basic requirements – the ability to direct and inspire a team, to set goals and monitor the progress towards these goals – are common to all such positions. Strong leaders remain strong wherever they operate, giving rise in most societies, to the development of *leadership networks*. Each of these networks consists of a very small élite, where the same names crop up again and again. They chair committees, sit on boards of directors, run charities, clubs and associations, as well as leading by example in virtually every walk of life.

One only needs to thumb through a few entries in *Who's Who* to see many examples of this. If you get to the top of your particular tree, people seek you out to join them, or to support them on theirs. Successful chairmen of companies can collect directorships the way lesser mortals collect stamps. Top skills are seen to be transferable, to everyone's benefit. Charities, for example, want top organization men and women as their patrons. They bring not so much their skills or their money, but their names, contacts and influence, better to raise funds for the begging bowls of life. Every serious public figure seems to have at least one charity or cultural good cause in his or her gilded c.v. The length of some *Who's Who* entries, with all their professional and voluntary appointments, raises questions as to how the individual concerned finds the time or energy to perform his or her central function.

One group of leaders who may have few if any management skills are moral or ethical leaders such as the ayatollahs, bhagwans, popes and archbishops, spiritual figures of all types and denominations and philosophers and thinkers. Such people have very subsidiary administrative roles and lead largely by example. While they may have clerical and lay organizations to back up the spiritual and social disciplines that they wish to see followed or imposed, that is not their main function. Similarly, intellectual leaders exist in most walks of life. Leading academics, surgeons, lawyers and artists lead not because they set out so to do, but because those in shared disciplines and careers wish to follow their example and emulate their skills. Such figures are leaders too, but with no established organization behind them. The great writers and dramatists of the twentieth century like George Bernard Shaw have influenced more than one generation, as Bertrand Russell has in philosophy, Henry Moore in sculpture or Picasso in art. They led because they were ahead of the field.

In business, financial and industrial life, too, practice can be entirely changed by individuals, be they J. P. Morgans or Andrew Carnegies. Lord Hanson and his lifelong partner Sir Gordon White have (and my view is shared by many) helped bring about a revolution in British management philosophy over the last two and a half decades.

But how do leaders get chosen? How do certain individuals make their special way to the top of the tree?

Chapter 5
Selection and Self-Selection

'Thank God only one of them can win.'
Car bumper sticker during the Bush/
Dukakis election campaign

'An American President is selected by the newspapers, which know little about him, by the politicians, who do not want a master but a slave, by the delegates to a national convention, tired, with hotel bills mounting, ready to name anybody in order to go home. The presidency, the one great prize in American public life, is attained by no known rules and under conditions which have nothing in them to make a man work hard or think hard, especially one endowed with a handsome face and figure, an ingratiating personality, and literary style.'
Mirrors of Washington Anon. 1921

The process of becoming a leader in any walk of life is largely to do with selection – either natural selection or selection by peers, by the electorate, by the would-be led, by the system. Many of the best leaders are chosen, by whatever process, from a short-list of one: there is no one else available of equal stature. But usually a choice has to be made.

Before the selection process can begin, the candidate has to present him or herself as being available. He or she has to have an ambition to lead, and has to take a positive decision to push themselves into the ring. Most potential leaders, after all, are not dragged kicking and screaming out of obscurity, digging their heels in to avoid serious preferment. They choose to allow their names to go forward. This is known as 'I'm here-ism'. You don't have to be pushy but you have to get noticed, preferably by what you do more than by what you say. Those who hide their lights under bushels for too long can see the fire extinguished. The oxygen of exposure, of recognition, is essential. I have often seen good candidates for preferment, in the diplomatic service and in business, ignored because they were invisible, with their heads always well below the parapet for modesty or other reasons. You have to stand up and say 'I am a candidate. I am a good candidate. This is why.'

Why do they act in this way? What drives men and women to want to become leaders? It is not enough merely to talk about ambition. Among the largely selfish goals and rewards that they seek will be:

1 Financial recognition, though this is by no means the primary goal, particularly for those attracted to public service positions.

2 Non-financial rewards: titles, decorations, free housing, cars, chauffeurs, etc; simple hedonism – a wish to live better.

3 Self-satisfaction or self-esteem: the fulfilling of

Freudian ego-goals (as opposed to catering to mere ego) towards which we all consciously or unconsciously strive. (We will probably change or keep moving these goals to provide constant challenge.) For a lot of people power is a great aphrodisiac and with esteem comes sexual attractiveness, which many consider no bad thing.

4 Status: the need to make a mark for posterity. The might and reputation of some leaders long outlasts their demise, whether they set out to achieve this or not. Thus Mao Tse-tung's ideological leadership for long remained unquestioned by the Chinese people. He achieved his pre-eminent status after the 'Long March', but his *Little Red Book* containing his thoughts effectively became the moral law of the country.

5 More leadership, power or influence: continuation in office. They want to survive.

6 Overcoming frustration with the *status quo*: a genuine wish to change things. Leaders tend to enjoy what they are doing and some actually view it all as a great game. They have a desire to overcome the unerring desire of their fellows to be slothful.

7 Stretching and proving themselves through excitement, whether violent or peaceful. They seek out responsibility. History is littered, incidentally, with terrorists turned politicians, and nowhere

more so than in the Middle East. Figures on both sides of the Arab-Israeli divide, from Yasser Arafat to Menachem Begin, started their careers fighting with bomb and gun.

8 Certain general, non-selfish, worthy aims such as the wish for a better world or a more efficiently run company or golf club, or other political, social or economic ends. All-embracing Renaissance Kings such as the French François I and some of the English Henrys are examples of this: they were involved in all aspects of life, not just government and war, but also science, architecture, education, religion and the arts.

Against all these plusses, would-be leaders will weigh up the disadvantages, and in a media-dominated society they are many. The self-evident burdens of leadership include:

1 Lack of privacy.

2 A truncated family life – though successful leaders tend to find strategies to protect their families.

3 Long hours of work.

4 Fear of public failure (the media in every country love coming down from the hills and shooting the politically wounded).

5 Health / stress factors: they will have to watch

their diet and their life-styles.

6 The pressure of people trying constantly to influence them for reasons of their own. Incessant
lobbying and demanding of favours by others is a
very time-consuming part of leadership life.

These are serious drawbacks for people who might
otherwise offer themselves for future high rank. There
are many documented cases, particularly in the United
States, of well-qualified individuals deciding against
running for high office, right up to and including the
presidency, because of the horrific strains such a process of election puts on self, family and friends. Many
of the best don't run, if only because it can be very
lonely on the top of the leadership mountain.

By and large, therefore, a joint act of will is required
between candidate and selectors. The candidate puts
him or herself forward, and may then be chosen by one
of several processes: by a predecessor in the leadership
office, as when General Franco chose King Juan Car-
los; by a selection team; by a wider democratic process;
or by some less rational process of struggle, which we
might call the law of the jungle or the smoke-filled
room syndrome.

Some leaders, however, have had unexpected levels
of greatness thrust upon them. As Enoch Powell has
written, more than any other eminent position, that of
prime minister is filled by a fluke. Stanley Baldwin, for
example, became prime minister only because of the

fatal illness of Bonar Law. His leadership skills developed during his time as Ramsay MacDonald's deputy and as premier, and he grew adept at defusing unhappy situations such as the General Strike and the abdication crisis without too much long-lasting anger and bitterness. He was a mediator *par excellence*. Other leaders come to high office through assassination. Lyndon Baines Johnson and President Mubarak of Egypt were both relatively unknown when they replaced their popular and courageous predecessors, Presidents Kennedy and Sadat. With greatness thrust suddenly upon them, both grew into their unexpected roles, though Johnson's triumph in getting the Civil Rights Bill passed was overshadowed, in the judgement of history, by his ever-increasing involvement in the Vietnam war.

CROSS-TRANSFERENCE OF LEADERSHIP

'All rising to a great place is by a winding stair'
Francis Bacon

Before an individual sets out to climb the leadership ladder he or she has to identify what that ladder is leaning against, and to realize that there are many ladders leading to the top. Climbing one ladder in life may lead to a very unexpected leadership position. Thus a senior civil servant may become chairman of a merchant bank or a politician may move on to head some great arts or charitable foundation. For when a leader is being head-hunted the selectors go for the general quality and leadership potential of the individual, rather than for their specific skills in or experience of the area concerned.

Recent chairmen of some of our biggest companies and institutions have been brought in from outside because they were the best pure leaders available. They brought with them a breadth of experience and vision that was perhaps lacking among candidates who had spent their working lives in the organization. This cross-transference at the top also tends to happen because new brooms are believed to sweep cleaner and more tellingly than old. Lord Carrington, former High Commissioner in Australia, former Defence and Foreign Secretary, former Secretary-General of NATO, is now chairman of Christie's International. He is a classic example of those old Etonian/Sandhurst figures who still occasionally come to the fore, with effortless superiority (as they used to say of Balliol men), to take charge of whatever organization comes into their view.

It is interesting to look briefly at other similar examples of this ability to switch leadership from one field to another totally different one. The gifted newspaper proprietor, Lord Beaverbrook, moved on to serve – with vigour, dedication to detail and success – first as Minister of Information after the First World

War, and then as Minister in charge of Aircraft Production in the Second World War. Dwight Eisenhower, acquired the highest of profiles as Commander-in-Chief of US Forces in Europe during the Second World War, which he perpetuated after the war when he became Supreme Commander of NATO forces in Europe. Such a heroic image ensured that once he had been selected as the Republican presidential candidate there could be no question of his leadership qualities, and he was returned with a triumphant majority.

Few, however, can rival the spectacular succession leadership positions held by one Jean Baptiste Bernadotte 1763-1844. His rise from the rank of private in the French army to field-marshal was not entirely exceptional. But he then moved on to become Napoleon's governor of the Hanse towns, where he was befriended, and then actually adopted by, the childless King of Sweden. He later succeeded to the thrones of both Sweden and Norway as King Charles XIV.

Is it really true that most leaders possess qualities which set them apart from ordinary mortals? Is there an elite personality type? Do such people really have similar traits, common characteristics, which allow them to move easily between roles? Certainly it does not always work. After all the Duke of Wellington, the 'Iron Duke', may have been a great military leader, but he and his skills translated badly to political life. In war he had never been obliged to compromise, and it was a habit he found difficult to acquire in his dealings with his parliamentary colleagues when he became prime minister.

A common factor that certainly does exist, however, is an *appearance* of leadership, a style of living and interacting with others. If leaders are good, they possess an *aura of competence*. In other words, though their individual personalities may vary greatly, other people's reactions have much that is shared. It is this reaction to a certain robustness of mind, a sense of mission, an inner drive, an ability to think big, that builds and creates leadership wherever it is found.

The flow chart below shows another way of looking at the whole process:

Leadership achieved

The electorate
makes its   →   ↑
choice
                                    Broadcasting
                              ←   of
                                    experience
Presentation to   and
wider electorate   responsibility
        ↑
Selection
process
        ↑
'LUCK'   Presentation to
or   →   'scrutineers'.
'opportunity'   selection committee
or
'openings'   ↑

Persuasion of peer
groups as to
personal merits
                                    Specialized
            ↑   ←   training and
                                    experience
Establishes
reputation:
The 'I'm here' factor

Early   Background,
incentive   →   ↑   ←   education,
                                     abilities
Candidate self-
selects for future
leadership role

THE SELECTION PROCESS

Selection processes vary, but groups and elites in every society have a variety of ways, formal and informal, of controlling access – initially to the groups themselves and then, more especially, to positions of leadership within those groups. They lay down requirements, written or unwritten, stipulating certain conditions of background, birth, education, or experience, controlled by interview or examination. Most groups organize the process of both entry and preferment with highly disciplined procedures carried out by specially created scrutiny or membership committees. Political parties have their democratic or closet systems just as churches have their colleges of bishops or cardinals. One widely imitated system for selecting future leaders is the 'mandarin method' used by many British Establishment organizations, including the Civil Service, an example being the old W.O.S.B. (War Office Selection Board).

The process developed out of the 'country house' system in which candidates were monitored over a period of a few days by a team of professional judges or adjudicators, and has many merits. Aspiring entrants were brought together to a house in the country to be interviewed, minutely watched and examined, not only on how they coped with the tests with which they were confronted, in order to see if they were fit to govern

India or other far-flung parts of the Empire, but also on their dress and behaviour. The much-mocked etiquette of manners mattered. It still does:eating peas with a knife will count against you. While the general method nowadays does not include any country house residence, the 'style' of the candidate is still important. The general method is to divide candidates into groups, or syndicates, of four or five, and to present them with issues and problems to solve both jointly and individually. Their handling of these cases is judged in relation to that of the other candidates, and marked in terms of leadership potential. Higher up the leadership tree, less obvious but similar methods of selection for preferment frequently prevail as men and women are filtered and tested for any given position. It is not, of course, mere intelligence that is being looked for in such a process. Future leaders are chosen for a whole range of reasons, but – again – as much for their appearance or for how they can be built up, as for how they really are.

THE CREATION OF A LEADER

Ad hoc methods sometimes have to be found for choosing leaders when a vacuum suddenly develops or a cause needs to be served quickly. The unexpected death or incapacity of the incumbent, or their involvement in scandal or some critical failure of leadership, brings crisis in its wake. The kingmakers, perceiving the need, quickly swing in to action and seek out a candidate who, with the right treatment, will present the best public persona. Such kingmakers always emerge to oversee the right choice at the right time. Sometimes the choice is inevitable; hence, for instance, Norman St John Stevas's remark when Margaret Thatcher was selected: 'It wasn't an election. It was an assumption.' Look also at the 'creation' of Ronald Reagan, president, from an ex B-movie star. Here was a man, all of whose simple talents were up-front, who was 'the best available at the time', who was there to be used and managed by those behind him for the sake of the Republican Party.

Around Reagan were many people with greater talents, and with potentially high leadership qualities, but who lacked the necessary access to a public platform, or the money, or, more crucially, who simply did not wish to shoulder the burden and responsibility of leadership, with its harsh exposure to the popular gaze. Reagan's choice as a presidential candidate was widely mocked by people like Jack Warner, who remarked ruefully, 'It's our fault: we should have given him better parts.' But it worked with the American people. Even the most successful presidents have to some extent been created. John F. Kennedy was just as much a president who was 'made': in his book *The Making of the President*, Theodore H. White, relates how the media was used to best advantage, and the image-makers set to work to ensure that Kennedy beat Nixon in 1960. Television electioneering had come into its own, and the media manipulators knew how to stage-light Kennedy and make him up so that he looked clean and clear-eyed, as opposed to Nixon, on whose brow sweat glistened, and whose five o'clock shadow made him appear as sinister and devious as he later turned out to be. There is no doubt also that Kennedy's posthumous reputation rests partly on the shocking circumstances of his death.

Even where there is a well-thought-out process of selection, it may be counter-balanced by an equally powerful inertia factor, giving rise, say, to a decision to make do with moving up an existing deputy leader in order to avoid trouble. Dead men's shoes are a common route to the top. Equally, many leaders are chosen not for their positive qualities, but − through the lowest common denominator (LCD) factor − because they arouse fewest disagreements about them and their qualities. Thus it is generally recognized that Michael Checkland was chosen as Director-General of the BBC in 1982 because the governors could not agree between several outstanding but controversial candidates such as Michael Grade, Jeremy Isaacs and Paul Fox. Such arguments run along the lines that Candidate X is too risky and Candidate Y is too controversial, so Candidate Z is picked even though he or she is widely judged to be as a less able character. The perceived future value of X or Y may be greater, but a calculation of the present 'opportunity cost' or opportunity foregone by not choosing Z makes it worthwhile in the context of the overall balance sheet.

We looked earlier at the qualities necessary for effective leadership. As an aside here it is worth mentioning that for some leadership positions too much intellectual ability and agility may actually be seen by the electors as a bad thing. People of outstanding intellect – the examples of Adlai Stevenson and Ian Macleod spring to mind – may be considered too clever by half where more straightforward or practical skills are thought to be required. Clear, simple beliefs (Thatcher, Reagan) may be considered best. As Jonathan Swift noted, 'When a true genius appears in this World, you know him by this sign: the dunces are all in confederacy against him.'

THE LEADERSHIP EQUATION

I tend to formalize the selection process in the following way: *becoming a leader rests on timing, circumstances and personal qualities*. Timing is crucial: an opportunity must arise at the right moment – this is often, as we have seen, a matter of chance or luck. Circumstances must be favourable: there must be a need for a new leader; the 'state of the nation/company' factor must come into play. And in the light of such circumstances, personal qualities come to the fore – energy, drive, and background, as well as expertise and other acquired skills. Hence the leadership equation:

T + C + P = Leadership

T, C and P are all weighted, and the correct combination will produce the right choice.

Of all these factors the most important is timing. History is littered with examples of leaders who come or rise to office at the critical moment. One leader whom the circumstances of time fitted to such perfection was Konrad Adenauer, first chancellor of the Federal Republic of Germany in the aftermath of the Second World War. A former mayor of Cologne, he was imprisoned by the Nazis but became mayor again after 1945, while at the same time founding the Christian Democratic Party. His wise but tough approach in dealing with the Allies, first as conquerors and then as partners, coupled with his fathering of the German 'economic miracle', was proof of his ability to build on defeat, to 'make good again', in the eyes not only of his fellow Germans but also of a wider world.

Timing can be thought of as gaining position through *windows of opportunity*. These windows are turning points or watersheds, the accidents of chance or lucky breaks that propel people up or down the career ladder or otherwise change their lives. How often do we hear people say, 'If it hadn't been for meeting him/being there/making that phone call/going to that dinner party/I wouldn't be where I am today'?

Such a window may prove elusive, even if you have all the necessary leadership qualities waiting to be utilized. And when it opens it may give access to one particular leadership position, even though other arenas might have suited the candidate better. To continue the analogy, there are, of course, windows that can be pushed open or even built, and opportunities that can otherwise be seized in order to reach the seat of command.

Once there, by whatever selection process, any leader is in the limelight — a crucial factor in the whole function of leadership.

Chapter 6
Leadership in the Goldfish Bowl

'They who are in the highest places, and have the most power, have the least liberty, because they are the most observed.'

John Tillotson

From a high political or social platform you have a commanding viewpoint from which to discern the direction in which people want you to go. But you are also highly visible up there. There is no escape from the public gaze. Hence one of the factors in the process whereby candidates with all the right qualities and qualifications are chosen: they put themselves forward for preferment. The selection process takes place by whatever method; the system, state, political party, industrial company, bank, educational institution or whatever chooses the individual who is perceived to have the potential to become a successful leader. Media appeal plays a critical part in this process, for it will be the leader's reputation in the market place that will become the measure of success or failure. Fame and the appearance of success feed themselves, and perception may be more important that reality. Image is the beginning and the end of good leadership. It is only when it outgrows reality too far that it can lead to disaster.

Goldfish are reputed to change size according to the size of their bowl. So it is usually with leaders: they are 'made' rather than 'born'. Consider Presidents Truman or Sadat or even Margaret Thatcher at the beginning of their careers, as they emerged from the shadows cast by their predecessors. Some pundits and star-gazers may claim otherwise, but by and large they and their qualities were difficult to detect before they came into public view. When an incumbent takes up office, the position itself very rapidly invests him or her with status. In 1974 the *Guardian* newspaper joked: 'A year ago Gerald Ford was unknown throughout America; now he is unknown throughout the world.' But within the embrace of office even Ford grew in stature and ability. This in part was due to the oxygen – or cyanide – of publicity, with which, from day one, all leaders are surrounded. Here again, unless the commentators and opinion-formers are particularly sharp, image may win out over substance. As I write this chapter, for example, the lack-lustre, wimpish Vice-President Bush is being transformed by the system and by public perception into a figure who stands far taller than the man himself. That is the nature of leadership: it can surprise even the incumbent, who may not have realized that the necessary qualities lay latent within.

Leaders are constantly exposed to the public gaze, and are seen to succeed or fail on the public stage. Invisible leadership may work in certain commercial and industrial circumstances, but not in political life, where good or bad points are frequently awarded according to public perception rather than reality. A good reputation as a leader is hard to dent. A bad reputation lingers long. If John F. Kennedy was made President by good public relations, Richard Nixon was destroyed by lack of them. Long before them both, Abraham Lincoln was an outstanding manipulator of public opinion in order to serve his political ends. Perhaps the greatest of all American Presidents, and with the greatest role to play in a country divided by civil war, he had a clear vision of the future, where he saw a united nation, reconciled, 'with malice towards none; with charity for all . . .' He knew about goldfish bowls.

There is not just one goldfish bowl; there are many. In the eyes of his peer group, if he has one, a leader may be all reasonableness and ability. To those below him or watching from the wings, however, he may be quite the reverse. Similarly a leader who is popular among his followers may, by contrast, emerge as highly inadequate when exposed to his peers. Any commentator on political summits will acknowledge the truth of this.

The leader is always in front of the cameras. What they say and do is analysed minutely. Often a mild statement becomes extreme, because fact is embellished and truth is exaggerated. Good leaders play the media game. They recognize the simple rule: *a reputation for good leadership creates good leadership.*

In other words, leaders grow into their reputation. Long before the days of mass communication the first Duke of Marlborough built up a justified reputation as a military leader in the war against France. But his greatest strength lay in the image his men had of him. He was personally both greedy and acquisitive, and he changed his political stance on several important occasions, but he never forgot that his military standing depended on loyal troops, for whom he consequently always ensured the best possible wages and terms and conditions of service. Theodore Roosevelt believed that successful leaders were those who said what everyone else was thinking most often and in the loudest voice. These are the reasons why in any modern society power struggles so often centre on the control and manipulation of the communications media. The Harold Wilsons and Norman Tebbits of this world, themselves expert in manipulation, are the first to cry foul when they feel the media are sceptical. The people who come over best on television screens and through newspaper headlines are those who, to misquote Laurence Olivier, believe that if you can fake sincerity you can fake anything. They win out over those who struggle over mere matters of policy in backrooms because they are more practised at being convincing.

Yet who has changed their view of politicians following the televising of the House of Commons? In 1988 Mrs Thatcher observed, 'I do not think television will ever televise this House. If it does televise it, it will televise only a televised House, which would be quite different from the House of Commons as we know it.' How right she was. The stage has now grown by many thousands of times. Performance in the House is directed not so much at other MPs but at the editors of television news programmes. Visual 'sound bites' are becoming the order of the day. The carefully argued speech is disappearing, because it cannot easily be edited down to twenty seconds.

As we have seen, political parties in the democracies, if they are wise, choose their leaders according to their ability to come across well to their members, the media, the electorate, and a wider community, rather than their purely political skills. Great oratory, the ability to convince the mob, has been a requirement of all leaders from the days of Demosthenes, one of the great speechmakers of the ancient Greek world. An electrifying presence at the rostrum or in front of the microphones and massed cameras is effective like nothing else in the political world.

The more important the leadership position, the wider the audience or electorate to whom an appeal must be made. The chairman of a small company may have to heed the views of and his standing with only a very few people – a couple of colleagues, the bank manager and one or two senior employees perhaps. By contrast, the boss of a large business will have to project himself not only to his peers but also to the wider business community, to government, to the media, to financial institutions and large investors, to shareholders, to customers, to the workforce and to the public at large.

It is an axiomatic that in order to gain a reputation for leadership you need one thing in addition to the above: endurance. Queen Elizabeth II and King Hussain of Jordan, for example, have acquired their skills and their standing by remaining on their thrones for well over three decades each – much longer than any other brand of leader in other walks of life. Monarchies, incidentally, have the advantage over presidencies of not having to inspire a multitude of platitudes every four or five years.

Everything a leader is or does is taken apart and analysed by those outside. Leadership is encouraged, allowed to atrophy or destroyed by public opinion, which in turn is fuelled by the media, who may report with detached interest, encouragement or scorn. Negotiation between leaders, of management and unions for example, is often frustrated by public exposure. This leads to the over-simplification of arguments and consequent hardening of negotiating positions, when undercover subtlety is what is really required. As leaders have followers, it is difficult for them to admit to changing their minds or being wrong. Some accidental slip – President Ford's repeated stumblings, for example – will mark a leader a hundred times more strongly in the popular mind than any number of carefully drafted public utterances. When President Carter was seen collapsing while jogging his image as a strong or effective leader suffered enormous damage. Unjust and unfair, but true.

In addition to the primary rule that reputation creates leadership, there are three other *goldfish bowl rules*:

1 Flexible leadership decreases as exposure increases. The more you have to state your case in front of the television cameras, the more set that case has to become. You cannot bend or change it, particularly in reaction to opposition criticism, without accusations of having done a U-turn, backed down or whatever. The more delicate the negotiation and the more insecure your case, the more you need to avoid exposing it in order to keep your future flexibility out of the public eye.

2 Political (and, to an increasing extent, business) leadership is one long press conference.

3 The real standing of a leader is in inverse proportion to the number of PR staff needed. Good leaders do not need silly-statement-repair teams, who arrive after the verbal catastrophe to announce, 'What the President meant to say was . . .'

At the international level there used to be differences between nations as to how much public/media attention mattered to their political leaders. The Americans have long been alert to the need for leaders to respond well to the media, Britain now follows close suit, and recently we have seen the Soviet Union, in the figure of Mikhail Gorbechev, make moves in the same direction. The Kremlin's public affairs spokesman, Gerradi Gerasimov, makes the White House equivalent, Marlin Fitzwater, look very ordinary indeed.

I have had the opportunity to study at close hand some very inadequate people in the guise of leaders. They have got away with it because their window-dressing, or more particularly their window-dressers, have been good. At worst, such a situation is like the protective layer which his staffers built around the geriatric Churchill in his last years in office, or around the clinically dead Brezhnev in his latter period in the Kremlin. I am fascinated by the way these manipulators manage to create and sustain leaders from the sparsest raw materials. The prime leadership rule is: who presents well, wins.

Chapter 7
The Image Makers

'Greatness in the presidential chair is largely an illusion of the people.'

Time magazine

Image-builders know that the most cynical among us, the most intelligent, the most politically mature, are like children when it comes to assessing our fellow men and women. We may deny it, but we are all over-whelmingly influenced by first impressions. Looks, dress, bearing and initial utterances are deeply etched in our memory and judgement, and the view we form in the first fifteen seconds is not easy to dislodge. Re-assessing and overcoming our initial prejudice is a long process; indeed we tend to distort subsequent sightings in order to reinforce our first, instant reaction.

In the USA seventy-five per cent of the electorate at the 1988 election said that they would vote for the next president on gut feeling, which is much the same thing. Life is too busy and too short to suspend judgement for long. Of the two presidential candidates one was seen as a dull little man; the other as an amiable wimp. No matter what their policies were or which underlying qualities they could bring to office, voters made up their minds not because of what Bush or Dukakis said, but because of how they said it.

They set aside the fact that Bush had been a distinguished officer in the war, that he had been director of the CIA, and ambassador to the UN and China – jobs in which, admittedly, he appears to have made little mark. They set aside Mr Dukakis's long, worthy but less well-known career in Massachusetts. They looked only at the present, the here and now. Dukakis was well-versed but boring and wooden. Bush was less assured, more prone to verbal stumbles, and had a funny grandmotherly voice which was even worse until he learned to drop the pitch. Neither was perceived as particularly 'presidential', neither stirred the heart of the nation with his language or style. Bush stood taller by a head, which mattered in different ways to different people. Taller equals nicer? Smaller equals more powerful and aggressive? Most electors made an instant judgement about which of them *looked as if* he was more human and had a sense of humour. Which was why Bush was to win.

I have developed this example to prove one thing. I am not arguing that some individual policies and in particular the overall judgement of the candidates, was not taken into account by the electorate, but only that the latter formed a very cursory and rapid view. The budget deficit, and arguments on defence spending, foreign policy, or even crime and violence persuaded relatively few voters one way or another. But the candidate's way of arguing his case did. For example, Dukakis's mishandling of questions on abortion was widely reported; instead of showing some human feeling when asked what he would do if his wife were raped, he responded with a little homily on crime prevention. That did nothing to capture the important women's vote – or anyone else's for that matter.

In any leadership struggle, as in an election, the main protagonists have media advisers, PR consultants, advertising strategists and speech-writers. They also have campaign managers though British candidates must be seen to be actively heading their campaign teams. In the American system, by contrast, the Bonar Law syndrome – 'I must follow them, I am their leader' – too often prevails. Campaign directors and media advisers decide. Because of the geographical extent of the country and the lack of truly national newspapers, the televisual image is the key to presidential elections. The candidate is therefore wheeled here and there at the behest of the image-builders.

Candidates are commodities to be packaged and presented by the teams around them. Everything must be manipulated, made up, and lit to look good on television. The sound must be right as well. Sound bites must be practised to perfection. Speeches are made not in order to inform but rather as a PR exercise. In the race to the top it is once again the best televisual image, not platform or policy, that produces the winner.

Leaders in all walks of life are presented, inflated, promoted or apologised for by the team of media handlers around them. Following the Reykjavik Summit in 1986 Donald Regan explained their role: 'Some of us are like a shovel brigade that follow a parade down Main Street cleaning up. We took Reykjavik and turned what was really a sour situation into something that turned out pretty well.'

President Reagan's frequent verbal gaffes were explained away particularly effectively by his press office, and the White House press corps, by and large, let the fairy story go on even after such howlers as 'trees are a major cause of pollution'. If the President said something wrong it was up to everyone concerned not to mock but to cover up. The emperor must always have new clothes.

Why was he protected? His PR people long knew the answer. He was Mr Nice Guy, the Teflon President on whom nothing nasty would stick. He appealed to the mid-West, even if he was not always too bright on issues or often seemed detached from the realities of his job. He mastered the trick: in his leadership, like all leaderships, the one key selling point was what really counted. The campaign team's job was to market the product on that basis, whatever the reality.

Those concerned with creating image know how important it is for the reputation and success of individual leaders, just as it is for causes or organizations. While substance and the real value of a case must be well established, when argued in public that substance always takes second place to how the case is argued and by whom. As Daniel Boorstin wrote, 'Shakespeare, in the familiar lines, divided great men into classes: those born great, those who achieve greatness, and those who have greatness thrust upon them. It never occurred to him to mention those who hire public relations experts and press secretaries to make themselves look great.' The in-group expression in the States is 'savvy handlers', the people who save the Dan Quayles from themselves – and doing it badly in his case. They make them look more human, wiser, more skilled. Presentation to the media is all.

In PR much depends on the perceived qualities of the individuals who are to be promoted or the individuals leading the organizations that are to be promoted. Some leaders are very capable of presenting themselves, but other equally brilliant leaders come across badly on television, since it demands a different type of skill. At their best, the media sees through hype and insincerity. This is why there has developed a very active mini-service industry, a sort of public relations charm school network, which will take your would-be leader, your up-front man or woman, and teach them all the tricks of the trade. Acting is a useful leadership skill. 'Delivery, delivery, delivery is everything,' said Demosthenes. No one can wave a wand and make a poor speaker a great orator, but they can make them passably effective. A fumbling, inarticulate shambles of an interviewee can be turned into someone who knows their limitations and who can put a case across without too many problems.

On the public platform and on the television screen, as in any other encounter, the first fifteen seconds are crucial. Thus dress, posture, appearance and opening words must match the occasion. If the subject dresses shabbily or speaks with a lack of clarity or assurance, they will be perceived as indecisive and run down unless their reputation is otherwise established. It is a matter of teamwork: the marionette and the puppet-master work as one in the image-creation game. In some extreme cases (for instance in some inherited positions) appearances are all that stand in the way of oblivion, since apart from image there is nothing else there. The savvy handlers build even when there is almost nothing there. Take Mr Quayle again. They will get the camera angles right. The still pictures will express might and greatness – as with the ones chosen by the *Independent* to illustrate Margaret Thatcher's towering superiority over her colleagues at the 1988 Conservative Party conference.

In the political world, though less so in industry and commerce, the handlers can end up almost more important than the candidates themselves: Michael Deaver and James Baker in the White House are but two examples. Speech-writers like the legendary Peggy Noonan, who worked for Reagan and then for Bush, produce the 'script' and all the 'leader' does is read his or her lines. As she has written: 'The battle for the mind of Ronald Reagan was like French warfare of World War I: never have so many fought so hard for such barren terrain.' By their words, by what they say or are reported to have said, are they known. Success is measured by the length of standing ovations. Great care is consequently taken over the words a leader is to utter, from the keynote speeches to be delivered to party conferences to the briefs that civil servants prepare for ministers, or the prompt cards that President Reagan had for his every minor interview in the Oval Office.

In the old days leaders were believed to write their own speeches. Whether this was ever true or not, in the mid-1960s Harold Wilson was able to mock the then Prime Minister, Sir Alec Douglas Home, by revealing that Eldon Griffiths and Nigel Lawson actually wrote his speeches for him. Now it is an accepted fact of political life. Colour and jokes and memorable phrases are created along with the substance. Douglas Hurd cut his teeth writing words for Edward Heath, and today a team including the playwright Sir Ronald Millar produces scripts for Margaret Thatcher. The bond is tight between wordsmith and speaker. The latter reaps the glory or the blame.

Chapter 8
Leadership Styles

'It is personalities not principles that move the age.'
Oscar Wilde

There are two extremes of operating style: the totally autocratic and the fully consultative. I call them the *go and do* and the *come with me* approaches. In the real world most leaders adopt a style somewhere in between.

```
          Autocratic              Consultative
                     A        B
Dictatorship ←————————————————————→ Anarchy
          Individual              Collective
          leadership             leadership
          (e.g. Prime Minister   (e.g. 'traditional'
          Thatcher's             cabinet
          government)            government)
```

Though Harry Truman followed Machiavelli in believing that the only efficient form of government particularly in the times of national danger, was a dictatorship, in the end a pure autocracy destroys itself. At the opposite end of the spectrum a properly collective leadership merges into feeble 'government by committee'. There is no doubt that in most circumstances the range A to B on the spectrum is best, where the leader leads, but as executive chairman (as Harold Wilson called the job of prime minister), also consults and takes advice.

Pure management by committee, which requires constant whitewashing to ensure the public appearance of unity, has few advocates. Neither does anyone want a leader with no checks and balances on their actions. Hence the debate about the Thatcher style of leadership. One of the British prime minister's ultimate weapons is patronage, the ability to make appointments, to hire and fire. If taken to extremes, this can, consequently, lead to the appointment of puppets, sycophants and yes-men, the 'one-of-us-team' that does only what the leader says and wants. Thus are the normal checks and balances weakened.

Another way of looking at the same thing is to consider the spectrum from highly interventionist to laissez-faire. The highly interventionist type is usually a loner, and if unchecked can become a real nuisance and a hindrance to decision-taking at practical levels. Such individuals depend on no one. They tend to believe that only they can decide; they have a considerable opinion of their own importance and know their work to be crucial; they are reluctant to accept that they can be wrong. It is often a matter of face. They may camouflage or disguise this style by pretending to consult and listen, but they deceive nobody. They tend towards megalomania and often suffer heart attacks in the end.

A further danger of the highly involved or autocratic leader (or indeed any 'strong' leader) is that their underlings become increasingly dependent, and may become so conditioned as to be unable to take decisions themselves. The staff forget how to accept responsibility. *Autocracy breeds mediocrity down below.*

Critics of Margaret Thatcher's unique style of leadership accuse her of this. I am not sure she is a very good example in that she does delegate a large number of matters very effectively and efficiently to her ministers and civil servants. There are lots of better cases. David Owen, for example, has a tendency to consult and listen to no one: he is not a consensus politician. Sir John Junor, when he edited the *Sunday Express*, ruled absolutely. Those under him bowed or broke, as he himself had experienced under one of his first bosses, Beaverbrook. But both these men encouraged talent and there was a thread of rationality running through their autocratic leadership style. It is something that comes to affect many newspaper editors and proprietors, though often, as in Robert Maxwell's case, there is no safety valve, and opposition is not just stifled but eradicated on what often appears to be an irrational whim.

All men would be tyrants if they could, according to Daniel Defoe, and in the ruthless suppression of all national or personal opposition Stalin probably remains unsurpassed. His cunning, his lack of regard for

the rule of law or human life and his means of control –
the secret police – ensured a rule of and by terror. But
his mechanism for running Russia, except by terror,
was grossly inefficient and corrupt. Enlightened despotism has, however, had its place in history. Frederick
the Great of Prussia, with his marvellous political and
strategic acumen, coupled with his highly literary and
artistic background, possessed a range of qualities
necessary for the leader who was to forge Prussia's role
in a greater Germany.

Leaders verging towards the laissez-faire side of the
spectrum are often thought of as being good with their
immediate deputies. This is the team leader type, who
is willing to work on personal relationships. The autocrat, by contrast, will seek mass appeal, often doing so
over the heads of, or in direct opposition to, colleagues
and those closest to them.

Really effective leaders of both types have basic
goals like everyone else. *But these are not static.* Auto-
crats, particularly, will move the goal posts all the time.
They rewrite the rule book as they go, forging the conditions and circumstances that will give them and their
organization what they want, rather than accepting the
'givens' they encounter. Their personalities and their
skills allow them constantly to change gear. Weak consultative leaders, on the other hand, will destroy their
organizations much more quickly than any opposition
or competition can, simply by refusing to change without getting agreement from all concerned. Teamwork

is essential, but in the end one person has to decide.

There is a conundrum here. Some good leaders – that is those who are good at it – are inherently evil leaders. Unethical men frequently rise to high place. Hitler was a remarkable leader who used most of the tricks of the trade, managed change effectively, inspired his followers and so on. But all went to evil ends. He was an expert propagandist and an exploiter of human weakness and bigotries, who rose to power on a wave of anti-Semitism and anti-Marxism. His eloquence won him the most unlikely admirers, and his critics were silenced by fear of his SS and Gestapo. His was a classic case of the wrong person coming to power at a time of crisis and indecision, with disastrous results.

In my experience, a major mark of a good leader is not how hard they work but *how much they get done*. This is the principal rule that defines achievement and measures success. Most 'work' put in by average people advances matters not at all. Activity rarely equals effectiveness. Bustle in an office may be only bustle. Identifying the useful part – separating the wheat from the chaff, *then throwing the chaff away* – is the most difficult but rewarding aspect of political, business and social leadership. Even great leaders fall down through being unable to delegate or to leave detail to those with time to deal with it, by being unable to see the wood for the trees. In business, as in life, people can be measured by what takes up their time and what makes them angry.

Attention to some detail does matter. The best will attend to one fundamental detail – *that their subordinates should be well chosen to attend to detail*. As I said earlier, leaders with style recognize the dangers, which good managers often do not, of continuing to run or manage old, tired ideas and practices. They are animators, managers with added vision. They are like conductors of great orchestras who not only know the score and the musicians but can add an extra ingredient of their own. They know also, to continue the metaphor, that you can't lead the band if you can't face the music.

Wise leaders realize that for most of the time, in most of their areas of responsibility, they are not leading. Despite everything I have said about image, there are of course occasions when leaders lead best when people hardly know they exist. You don't always need to stand high on a platform and harangue the crowd in order to lead. Quiet command passed on through deputies can be a very efficient way of operating. Or of course you can lead via the puppet on the stage. I have seen the curtain that hangs behind the great couch-throne of the emperors of China in the Imperial City. The dowager empresses and others sat behind, concealed, whispering their commands through the draperies to the man-god in the seat of apparent power. Henry Miller once remarked that sometimes the real leader 'has no need to lead – he is content to point the way'. His or her style is to give others the direction, the conviction and the will to do what they want them to do. They are at the head of the pack, organizing the rest of us in the direction in which we are already heading. At worst they are what I call wet-finger leaders. They wet their finger then hold it up to see which way the wind is blowing before acting. They are the opposites of a Mrs Thatcher, who would never bow to the wind of mere popular opinion. Therein lies her strength and her weakness.

Whatever their style, leaders need to keep on top of things by following the *seven key controls of leadership*:

1 Control the mission. Keep that clearly in front all the time.

2 Control the execution of that mission.

3 Control the timing.

4 Control the people to make sure things are followed through.

5 Control the process of delegation down through the ranks.

6 Control the means of communication and information flow.

7 Above all, control yourself.

How these are weighted depends on circumstance. Let us look at that next.

Chapter 9
Crisis and Non-Crisis Leadership

'A leader or a man of action in a crisis almost always acts sub-
consciously and then thinks of the reasons for his action.'
Jawaharlal Nehru

The leadership skills needed for normal everyday life
are very different from those required in crisis situations. By and large, the captains and kings rise to great
things because great circumstances are thrust upon
them. Meaner, harder leaders are required. Those who
are successful in times of peace do not necessarily have
sufficient character to meet the very different challenges of war. Crisis leaders and leadership skills often
do not emerge until the crisis itself does. Weaker men
are then deflated by tension; moderate leaders are
pushed aside. Henry Asquith, the British Prime Minister and leader of perhaps the most gifted government
of the last hundred years (it included Churchill and
Lloyd George) brought in a major and far-reaching
programme of social and economic reforms in the
years up to 1914. But public faith in him waned in the
war years, the brilliance of his Liberal government's

achievements was quickly forgotten, and he was ousted in favour of Lloyd George who, it was widely felt, was better able and prepared to marshall the necessary resolve and resources to win the war.

The reverse process occurred after 1945, when Churchill, the war lord, was replaced by Clement Attlee, the mediator and moderator, who ushered in the welfare state and gave half the British Empire its independence. Churchill, by contrast, was seen by the electorate as a leader whose methods and experience did not fit him for the compromises that peacetime would require.

War and the shadow of war bring to the fore leaders who are more than the clichéd images of Biggles-like, outward-bound, military figures, or up-and-over-the-top, blue-eyed, sword-waving subalterns, followed by a devoted soldiery. War produces inspired leadership. But why? Because, as with other crises in political, economic, commercial and social life, it creates a situation where:

(a) the slow-moving 'natural' progression up the tree of command is questioned, and consequently,

(b) more people are *given the chance* to move rapidly up to leadership positions;

(c) bad leaders cannot be tolerated for long; and

(d) failed leadership is quickly overthrown.

In times of crisis, people will more easily follow a

single-minded leader who is an autocrat or dictator. Firm and speedy decision-taking, which a dictatorship allows, is seen as an absolute requirement, and many want to see the iron frame of custom broken by people of ardour and aggressiveness. When the crisis is over, however, resentment, opposition and hostility to that autocracy will grow rapidly: consider how the electorate reacted to Mrs Thatcher before, during and after the Falklands War.

I have always found crisis leadership to be the most interesting and exciting area of study in this field, largely because it leads to certain patterns of activity.

1 Adversity is a great selector of leaders.

2 Adversity is the ultimate test of leadership.

3 The greater the threat (to a nation, a government, a company) the greater the powers a leader can take.

Returning to the example of Mrs Thatcher and the Falklands crisis, she had the additional advantage of being *in situ*. Until the crisis erupted she was going through a very unpopular phase. Her standing was extremely low in national opinion polls, but she had already demonstrated at least some of her leadership skills. One could argue that as a result of the crisis, she had an element of 'greatness thrust upon her', gaining in stature and strength to such a degree that she was able to stand firm and get her own way in cabinet for many years thereafter.

In crises where there is a common enemy, people need not only leaders but also heroes, people to look up to, to rely on. They may well invest such heroes, with or without justification, with superhuman qualities. From the brave and gallant captain of a company of infantry-men to the Field Marshal, military hero-leaders are necessary for eventual victory, just as the company that wins in modern industrial takeover battles tends to have a highly powerful and charismatic helmsman. Whatever the outside world may think of them, many of their immediate colleagues would testify to the cha-rismatic qualities of men such as Tiny Rowland and Rupert Murdoch. They get things done quickly and effectively, using a mixture of charm and ruthlessness, backed by great innate skill, that inspires loyalty and brooks no argument.

Military leaders come in various styles: there are those who are known principally for one particular deed or victory, such as the Roman warrior Agrippa who defeated the fleet of Antony and Cleopatra at Actium, thereby cementing the power of the Roman Empire. There are heroines like Joan of Arc, who led her God-given campaign to free France from the English, dressed in armour like any soldier and cloaked with what appeared to her devoted troops to be divine radiance. That she was eventually betrayed by the Bur-gundians and sold to the English, at whose hands she was burned at the stake, only added to her reputation as a great national leader.

Military leaders may also become symbols of security to a beleaguered nation. Allied leaders – Montgomery, Eisenhower, Alanbrooke and others – assumed such mantles in the Second World War. The Israeli military commander and later Minister of Defence, Moshe Dayan, was a similar cult figure to the majority of Israelis for over three decades after the foundation of the state of Israel. Rebels may also be popular, like Orde Windgate, the leader or the irregular 'Chindits' in the Far East, or Field-Marshal Rommel, the good guy of Germany's war.

Montgomery defined military leadership as, 'The will to dominate, together with the character which inspires confidence. A leader has got to learn to dominate the events which surround him; he must never allow these events to get the better of him; he must allow nothing to divert him from his aim; he must always be on top of his job, and be prepared to accept responsibility.' He went on to say, 'These qualities are probably possessed in some degree by all men chosen as leaders, but they need to be developed by training; and they must be so developed throughout the Army. We must analyse the good and bad points in a man's make-up; we must then develop his good points and teach him to keep the bad points in subjection.'

He was astute in pointing out that the bad characteristics need to be controlled. The danger is that out of military circumstance dictators may be born, people who, to quote the Hindu proverb, 'ride to and fro upon tigers from which they dare not dismount'. Tyrants like Generalissimo Franco, civil war leader turned despot, manage to hold on to power by imposing the measures and regulations of war on a peacetime population.

LEADERSHIP IN NON-CRISIS SITUATIONS

'Anyone can hold the helm when the sea is calm.'
Publius Syrus

Non-crisis leadership requires different skills. In circumstances less critical than war, leaders tend to arrive or be promoted to leadership much more slowly. Natural progression is sluggish and bad leaders are tolerated for longer. In commercial life, for example, if the edge of competition is blunt and a company is complacent because it is doing all right, there is less of a struggle on the way to the top of the heap. Promotion will consequently be by traditional routes with everybody taking their turn on the steps of the pyramid of power. But such situations tend not to last too long amid the strains of threatened takeovers and mergers.

Where there is a lot of change in the air and the industrial/social climate is changing rapidly, political leadership has to match this by being flexible too. Strong political leadership conversely requires the private sector to match it in order to hold its own. But if there is no feeling of crisis, authoritarian, cold command won't work for long and leaders will have to try to influence, cajole or persuade, rather than order or command. Negotiation and compromise will be the order of the day in order to achieve balance between leader and led.

The consequence of all this is that while we do not want to have wars every time we want to throw up strong, single-minded and resourceful leaders, it is obviously better for any company or state to have a certain amount of stress and strain around to allow the most able people to emerge. The best-run organizations, consequently, will make sure that nothing stagnates, that challenges, opposition and constant striving for the top jobs keep everyone on their toes.

Competition is the ultimate creator and destroyer of leadership. As John F. Kennedy argued, opposition and rivalry within peer groups brings forward the best, the ablest, the ones with most allies. It's often called creative tension. This is not a case of dividing and ruling but of pitting people of often opinionated excellence one against the other, and extracting what is best from the resultant debate. Agreement between individuals can lead to rewarding progress; conflict can highlight risks and open windows of new thought, opportunity and initiative. Contrast this with dormant, lack-lustre situations, where all too often the nominal leader and the team around him or her will possess a lowest common denominator of talent, and will go for strategies that fewest disagree about. Out of such situations emerge prime ministers like Stanley Baldwin who, to quote Oswald Moseley, 'represented England asleep' being 'the Yawn personified'.

Where there is no conflict or crisis it is a common policy *to create one*, in order to cement support round a leader through the advocacy of some particular goal or mission. *Leaders need causes and causes need leaders.* Theodore Roosevelt put it soberly: 'The leader for the time being, whoever he may be, is but an instrument to be used until broken and then to be cast aside . . . the watchword for all of us is spend and be spent. It is a little matter whether any one man fails of succeeds; but the cause shall not fail . . .' One approach is to create a common enemy or threat in order to rally the troops or induce group loyalty. An opponent who threatens established order in war or in peace makes it easier for the leader to foster unity of purpose, on the lines of Benjamin Franklin's remark at the signing of the Declaration of Independence: 'We must indeed all hang together, or, most assuredly, we shall all hang separately.' When you have that group loyalty, you can then use it for other purposes. Thus Margaret Thatcher turned, fully strengthened, from the Falklands to beating the unions/inflation/over-bureaucracy/socialism or whatever.

And while we are on the subject of Mrs Thatcher, the history of the political world is surprisingly full of outstandingly successful women leaders. Elizabeth I possessed a perfect combination of leadership qualities, proven over a long period of time. A consummate politician, she could persuade her loyal subjects to act to her advantage without having to resort to official sanction. Broad-minded, she was able to defuse internal conflict and provide a more stable religious atmosphere. Human enough to inspire affection, yet distant enough to inspire awe and respect, feminine enough to inspire protection yet masculine enough to inspire admiration: it was a telling leadership mix. Female leaders have the handicap of usually having to work in male-dominated organizations. In reaction they often emerge as leaders of female causes. Emmeline Pankhurst is perhaps the best-known example in Britain. Eight times she went to prison in support of female emancipation, and each of her exploits, such as chaining herself to the railings of Buckingham Palace, enhanced her reputation among her followers.

In the latter part of the twentieth century, even in traditionally male-dominated countries, women leaders have not only reached pre-eminent political positions, but have also achieved outstanding things once they have got there. We need only think of Indira Gandhi or Benazir Bhutto or, in the Middle East, Golda Meier. Women leaders are present in many walks of social, economic and in many parts of the world, but particularly in Scandinavia. Britain is unique in having women as heads of both state and government, but why is it that in the world's greatest meritocracy, the USA, so few women have got anywhere near the top?

Women as leaders are no different: they need just the same qualities, qualifications, determination and sense of mission as any male. The only difference is that in order *to reach the leadership position, to beat male opponents or contenders, they need all these abilities and more.* Women, incidentally, move into despotism just as easily as men. Catherine the Great, despite many apparently liberal ideas, ruled with a rod of iron with and through the Russian aristocracy that surrounded and supported her.

Differences in leadership styles between various countries are more apparent than real. Germany, for example, has a reputation historically for autocratic leadership. South America today is still riddled with dictatorships, while the Scandinavians seem tradition-ally to favour rule by consensus. In reality, however, in any democracy much more depends on the character and personality of the leader than on any perceived national characteristic.

LEADERS OF THE SPIRIT

'As soon as I hear a leader talking about ethics, I know it is time to start counting the spoons.'

Variously attributed

Churches have the benefit of pulpits, from which priests are able to create gods and devils alike. Devils, in particular, help causes by uniting congregations against seen or unseen enemies. Spiritual belief of whatever kind is a unifying force of great strength. Many of the most famous spiritual leaders had little in the way of organizations to lead during their lifetimes. Leadership of this sort is provided by disciples and creeds long after the death of the central figure; such as Christ, Buddah or Mohammed. A different but in many respects similar phenomenon is found among the declining number of followers of Marx and Lenin. The man who stands supreme among Christian leaders is St Paul, who led the scattered churches that he established through his correspondence with them, and became the interpreter of the faith that was to become the wider Christian church.

At a later date, discipline both of self and of the others was the driving force behind St Ignatius Loyola, founder of the Jesuits, just as his contemporary, the great Protestant leader Martin Luther, urged on his flock when they broke away from the Church of Rome. Breaking the chains of traditional religious practice was also the motivation of the founder of Methodism, John Wesley. In the very strength of his beliefs he was not always a tolerant man, and in his open-air crusades to convert the working classes to his church he showed little time for the established order.

Many contemporary leaders combine political and religious power, such as the ayatollahs of Iran and the El Mahdis of the Sudan. Archbishop Makarios of

Cyprus was another such, while in central and southern Africa many black bishops and clerics of various denominations have found holy orders a stepping stone to political prominence: Archbishop Desmond Tutu is a well-known contemporary example.

To the list of such modern spiritual leaders must be added the unusual example of the Aga Khan, who holds this hereditary title as supreme leader of the Moslem Ismaeli sect. Part prince, part religious divine, the various holders of this title (in addition to being renowned racehorse owners) have also held high rank in other fields. The Aga Khan III, for example, was President of the League of Nations just before the Second World War.

Mother Teresa is another example of a spiritual leader, who inspires not only her own order of nuns but many others throughout the world by her example.

Chapter 10
Training for Leadership?

TRAINING FOR LEADERSHIP

'He who has never learned to obey cannot be a good commander.'

Aristotle

'The statue is already in the rock. My job is to cut away surplus stone.'

Michelangelo

I have always felt that spotting future leaders was rather like dipping a tumbler into the sea and then examining its contents in order to study ocean currents. You don't see much at first glance. Those with potential, who appear to sparkle, may be like those of whom George Burns remarked: 'Too bad the only people who know how to run the country are busy driving cabs or cutting hair.' Big voices all too often speak small thoughts. The Peter Jays of the world peak too early then disappear.

The oil company Exxon runs a leadership training

scheme. So do military machines throughout the world. Much, after all, can be done to improve what one is born with, though everyone is limited ultimately by intellectual and physical ability. This does not necessarily conflict with the common belief that there can be no training for real leadership other than the experience of leadership itself.

It is certainly true that we do not recognize great leaders until they have done the job. But from the experience of such leaders, particularly in industry, it is possible to extrapolate some elements in their training that are common to many of them. After all, the West Points and Sandhursts of the world exist by believing that leadership is something in which people can become skilled. A poll conducted by the American magazine *Fortune* in October 1988 found that some seventy-three per cent of chief executive officers of large U.S. corporations shared this view. While many of these were undoubtedly thinking of management rather than leadership training, I believe that there are certain leadership qualities or leadership capabilities in many people which can be discovered, brought to the surface, developed and put to use. Provided the training and experience is there (coupled with certain inherent qualities of stamina and intellect), many people when faced with challenges of leadership can rise to them, to produce extraordinary results.

Baden-Powell, founder of the scouting movement, fervently believed that hidden qualities could be brought out of people if they were caught young. From his experience as the defender of Mafeking during the Boer War came a desire to give young people the outdoor experience that would make them more independent. In his philosophy, qualities of leadership developed from the necessity to tackle special physical and mental challenges that were not always present in day-to-day life. The whole outward-bound movement follows a not dissimilar belief.

Conditions which may help to develop potential leaders include:

1 Early exposure to responsibility and self-reliance.

2 Early training in decision-taking.

3 Early training in the need to communicate.

4 Early training in dealing with setbacks; the experience of having expectation thwarted and have to overcome apparently insurmountable obstacles.

People can be given all these experiences artificially. The fourth may seem a strange element in leadership make-up, but survey after survey brings it into the equation as a real factor in development.

Many people, not just in the armed services, make their living from something called leadership training. This involves providing the candidates with:

1 Goals to aim at.

2 Tools to get there.

3 Planning strategies.

4 Practice exercises to prepare for the real thing.

5 Analysis of success and failure in order to help build future strategies.

Above all, these courses build on the individual's experience by persuading him or her to think clearly about aims and objectives and ways of achieving them. In so doing, they identify and bring out whatever qualities of leadership may be lying dormant. It is an age-old process: the young Alexander the Great was tutored in this way by none other than Aristotle, largely through disputations. Debating is a very useful way of clarifying complex matters and bringing out latent skills in the protagonists. If few leadership qualities emerge in the end, tutors may (with the cynicism that is prevalent throughout the image-creation industry) promote *the appearance of* qualities that may make their students acceptable as future leaders.

I am also convinced that physical training of the outward-bound variety, involving leading teams on expeditions and on sailing and mountaineering trips and so forth, can develop the skills necessary for leading in the boardroom as well, provided the basic qualities are there. The mountaineer Chris Bonnington believes particularly that leadership in physically adverse circumstances – the south-west face of Everest in his case – can be applied with great effect in more mundane circumstances. And that it can be taught. It is a matter of fusing the two elements – inherent ability and environmental pressures – in a way that is new to the candidate's experience, which can result in a new product – a good leader.

It is easy to dismiss this philosophy of 'cold showers and a tough life.' But in real life, leadership involves relationships with other people in times of stress, and this rugged 'brains plus physical challenge' approach undoubtedly brings out both the good and the bad in people at all levels. It is equally easy to dismiss concepts such as *esprit de corps*, but any business leader, just as much as any military leader, will stress the importance of team spirit, along with high morale and a belief and trust in the man or woman at the helm. Leaders trained in gruelling physical circumstances also get to know how to assess the members of their teams as well as learning how best to motivate them and to allocate them their distinct individual roles. One man or woman with exceptional abilities, when faced with exactly the same team previously run by a poor manager, can transform a company, a political party or even a country. A team can climb an impossible mountain if properly led.

Of the 'three C's' of leadership, Communication, Confidence and Charisma, the first two can be developed, as we have seen. Communication is all-important in terms of relating to the two areas with which the leader must keep excellent contact, the immediate staff and the organization as a whole. Confidence, too, can be acquired and built upon, both through practice and through tuition in, for example, public speaking and negotiating skills. If you don't have it thereafter then you shouldn't be running in the leadership stakes. Confidence in itself is subtly different from self-confidence, which can be a dangerous quality if not kept under close scrutiny. Too much of that can lead to accusations of being too-clever-by-half. Self-confidence does not necessarily inspire confidence in others.

Personal appearance can be and often is developed as a confidence-building measure. Tone of voice matters as well, as Harold MacMillan taught and Margaret Thatcher learned. People who are especially blessed with other necessary qualities may be able to rise above unkempt hair, ill-tied ties, unpressed suits. But it is foolish to risk it, as Michael Foot in his donkey jacket at the Remembrance Day Service discovered. On the other hand, Mahatma Gandhi rose above such fripperies with his simple home-made loin cloths. But generally dark suits suggest dignity and gravitas; light-suited figures suggest the opposite, and you have to be an American president or an Israeli war lord to get away with an open-neck shirt. Power-dressing works as part of the image game. Those training or aspiring to be leaders should remember the following rule: *Actors are cast for parts because they look right. So are leaders. They must learn this skill just as an actor does.*

The elusive quality of charisma cannot be 'learned', however. Charisma is much talked about and rarely defined. But most people agree that it is unteachable. The ability to inspire, to create a dynamic setting in which things happen and others want them to happen, is rare. The charismatic, and often highly egocentric, leader has an electricity about him or her which provides excitement and drive both to an intimate and to a wider audience.

Image-makers have long realized, however, that while one cannot learn to be charismatic, *those parts of a person's make-up which might serve as a charisma substitute can be developed to have most appeal to most people.* There are those whom the camera loves, but who pale into insignificance in the flesh. And vice versa. The truly charismatic, like Tito, Churchill or Gorbachev, rise above both.

Aspects of leadership can be learned, or *released through self-realization, a desire for self-fulfilment and, above all, the seizing and using of circumstances.*

Chapter 11
The Leadership Team

'Leadership – the ability to get others to do what they don't
want to do and like it.'

Harry S. Truman

The greater and more powerful the leader, the larger
the element of feudalism within their court. Advisers,
unofficial or official, work within a team whose function is to serve, and which exists only as long as the
leader does. They all have a common aim – to ensure
that they continue in office.

For the leader there are two initial rules as regards
leading the team:

1 Power does not create loyalty. But wise patronage
 can.

2 You may be able to lead, but to rule you need
 others to help you. Choose well.

In other words, while until now we have been looking
at leadership in terms of leading the whole state or
organization, in fact the function of the leader also has

to be much more direct than that. In particular, leadership is about heading the immediate back-up staff and the administrative structure, the secretaries and assistants in the outer office, the inner cabinet, the top of the management pyramid.

Leaders need institutions to back them up in any moves to reform or modernize. In the distant past, King Edward I saw the need for a body quite separate from the dukes, earls, knights and courtiers who surrounded him, and so formed a prototype parliament out of the Great Council. It also helped that he believed in government by consent and the general principle that there should be no taxation without consultation. Leaders need personal advisers. Cardinal Richelieu, for all his skills and powers as statesman and church leader, also needed personal moral support, which he found in the shape of the priest Père Joseph, the original *eminence grise*. In modern times the Thatchers, Bushes or Gorbachevs, the Iacoccas, Weinstocks or Hansons all need a personal and professional team to advise them, to back them up, and to act efficiently on the decisions they take.

Successful leaders are known by the quality of those around them. They will hire the best to advise and assist. A poor leader, or a good leader who has become bad, may be so because the leadership team has degenerated into a collection of sycophants, courtiers and time-serving paper-passers, who tell their leader only what he or she wants to hear. Bad advice is the greatest threat to leaders, as George III found, particularly in his dealings with the American colonies. In the end, it is the leader, and not his or her advisers, who reaps the historical blame, and it is poor mad George whose decisions are ever remembered as having led to the War of Independence.

Kwame Nkrumah of Ghana started off as an enlightened liberator of his country from colonial rule. But he too was badly advised, and became a slave to his own vanity. Gradually, assisted, or at least not resisted, by those around him, he slipped into extravagance and self-glorification, to such a degree that his overthrow in the 1966 coup became inevitable. More recently, the sycophants around ex-President Marcos of the Philippines or the ill-fated President Ceaucescu of Romania have led to their downfall as tyrants on their ridiculous thrones.

Look at any team and you will find out a great deal about the leader. Good leaders, according to Confucius, are easy to serve and difficult to please. That is, they will tolerate reasonable behaviour and be agreeable to work for, but to reap praise from them requires something exceptional in the way of achievement. Many industrial leaders today are 'good employers' in the sense that they are popular and thoughtful. To get the most out of their staff or workforce however they have to be grudging in paying bonuses unless they are properly deserved. For leadership requires not only vision and a strategy for achieving objectives, but also willing and inspired teams at various levels to do the leader's will. While mutual trust and respect is more important than mutual liking, there is a need for a shared vision within the leadership team and right down through the organization. It is not just the leader that must ensure that this happens. The whole team has to think and develop as one. The whole culture of a company or an industry should be influenced by the style and personality of the chairman or managing director, particularly if that person also founded the enterprise in the first place. Consider the position of men like Henry Ford, Andrew Carnegie or J. P. Morgan in the industrial history of the United States.

Leaders need back-up not just to carry out their orders, but also to advise them, to keep them up to date and well-informed, and to present them to the wider public. We looked earlier at speech-writers, the best of whom are much more than mere hacks. They are part of the team, improving the leader's image by putting the right words and phrases into their mouths, and not simply writing the words but also judging when and how it is appropriate to say what. This can involve putting wise words into a tired mouthpiece (Reagan) or strong words into a wimpish one (Bush), or caring words into an uncharitable one (Nixon/Thatcher). Good speech-writers clearly enter into their leader's style, but also know how to create and deploy resonance where none previously existed. They are not puppetmasters, but provide essential reinforcements in the battle to persuade.

Good leaders need to watch out. Chains of command in many big offices and organizations are often marked by plenty of chains and frighteningly little command. The longer the chains, the greater the danger that decision-taking may get caught up, with each and every link posing its own risk. And weak links always seem to have the power to hold things up more surely than strong ones.

This leads on to the leadership skill known as delegation, since merely issuing orders is not leadership. Richard Nixon's advice was not necessarily infallible, but he had something of a point when he said, 'I have an absolute rule. I refuse to make a decision that somebody else can make. The first rule of leadership is to save yourself for a big decision. Don't allow your mind to become cluttered with the trivia. Don't let yourself become the issue.' The last sentence contained its own irony in his case. In any event many people in positions of authority do, like Nixon, become the issue, whether they plan to or not. Sir Thomas More became the issue with Henry VIII, just as de Gaulle did with Churchill during the war and with many of the other leaders of Europe after it. More recently, Nigel Lawson, despite all attempts at camouflage, was undoubtedly more the issue than were his policies in his dispute with Mrs Thatcher during 1989.

There is no hard and fast line. Some excellent leaders are good delegators to excellent teams. Very occasionally, good leaders, unwilling to admit that they can do wrong, are incapable of delegating anything, and even the slightest detail has to be scrutinized and approved by them personally. But this is very dangerous. It naturally diminishes and eventually removes any authority and incentive from subordinates, who become totally unused to taking any decisions of importance.

Both delegating and not delegating works in the short term. Obviously, the bigger the system, the more essential is delegation, since the entire decision-taking process can so easily be brought to a halt if everything has to be authorized from the top. In the great monolithic empires of the Soviet bloc, no one could take decisions without a huge formality of clearance. Hence the old joke about Foreign Minister Gromyko, who when asked whether he had enjoyed his breakfast replied, 'Perhaps'. In the longer term, a leader who does not delegate weakens both his or her own position and the organization, by stultifying natural talent further down the pyramid of power.

The rules of knowing when to delegate are:

1 Delegate to those with whom delegation works.

2 Delegate and empower those below in a logical and consistent way.

3 Avoid the 'command in order to control' approach.

4 Provide incentives for deputies, by means of financial and other rewards, for real work and real success.

5 Give praise when praise is due.

But in the end it is always lonely at the top, no matter how much the burdens of decision-taking are shared. In the final event, some decisions cannot be doled out to others and the leader stands alone. Leaders in the end have to stand in front, particularly in a crisis. Then, to mix metaphors royally, the buck stops at the top of the pyramid.

TEAM LEADERSHIP

'The inevitable end of multiple chiefs is that they fade and disappear for lack of unity.'

Napoleon

Not to be confused with leadership of a team, team leadership exists in circumstances where a committee or board leads, rather than one man or woman, just as the notorious Troika led the Soviet Union after Stalin's death. Where there is such an overlap in responsibilities it usually leads to disagreements. Leadership by teams, where there is no one who is recognized as *primus inter pares* or first among equals, tends, in political as in commercial life, to be a sign of weakness with the lack of a Darwinian leader, the fittest and strongest, available to come to the fore. Consequently, it seldom lasts long. Equal colleagues are dangerous. The famous triumvirate of Caesar, Pompey and Crassus in ancient Rome lasted while they divided up the spoils of war, but began to show cracks immediately afterwards. The trouble with equal partners is that you have to take account of and accommodate them and their views in all your own thinking. Allies, similarly, are hostages to fortune, and those on whom a leader is too dependent weakens the leadership.

Equal partners never are equal. Human nature requires that one person comes to the fore. Anything else is unstable. *Good teamwork has to mean a good team doing what the leader of that team inspires and directs.* That's what Lee Iacocca found when he took over Chrysler. He soon put a stop to the situation that had prevailed, where warring barons in charge of various departments did their own thing, irrespective of the interests of Chrysler as a whole. He chose the right staff and bonded them. If they didn't bond they went.

SPOUSES

Strong leaders frequently lack unbiased opinion or advice because their underlings or employees are frightened of them. Spouses can be of great influence and support, and some even rival their leader-partner in their power for good or evil. The Lady Macbeths of the world come and go, helping to create the leader and then dragging him down. Remember Elena, the viciously unpopular wife of Romania's former Communist dictator, President Nicolai Ceaucescu. Remember Imelda Marcos, who manipulated her ailing husband in his latter days of power, negotiating directly with his political allies and advisers, often with scant reference to him, and amassing a massive personal fortune in the process.

The tragi-comic dual leadership of Juan Perón and his wife Evita, on the other hand, achieved a cult following even though they hardly provided an effective or efficient leadership for Argentina. Backed by organized labour, Juan was foolish in antagonizing the Roman Catholic church, but the flamboyant ex-actress Evita, or Eva, gained the women's vote, and together they survived by capturing the imagination of many throughout the world.

Throughout history, spouses – especially wives – have played their part in the leadership game. If they are personable, wives are always dragged in to help if they have something to offer. Raisa Gorbachev and Glenys Kinnock add sparkle to their husbands' stand on issues, and are copiously used. The intelligent and charming Barbara Bush will, in time, add considerably to her husband's stature, just as staffers in the Reagan White House felt that the opposite was true of the role and standing of Nancy.

Chapter 12

Leadership Renewal: Decline, Fall and Succession

'The final test of a leader is that he leaves behind him in other men the conviction and the will to carry on.'

Walter Lippman

The constant renewal of leadership, the threat of renewal of leadership, and the process by which this is achieved, are the keys to the development and well-being of any nation, society or industrial enterprise. Unfortunately, as Mr Lippman was doubtless very well aware, a great many leaders suffer from the *après moi le deluge* syndrome, the 'no one could possibly do what I have done, couldn't-care-less what comes after me' attitude.

Many organizations, indeed, *are* their leaders. The *l'état c'est moi* phenomenon may be observed in a political, social or industrial context. The death or departure of a great, industrious, powerful or charismatic individual such as the emperor Charlemagne, for instance, is seldom followed by the appearance of an equal as a successor. There are few contemporary examples of one great industrial giant being followed by another within the same organization.

Political leaders, when they fall, tend to disappear almost without trace. They have done the job. Surprisingly, many if not most of them do not know or realize when and how to quit. But they go. They go on to happy or bitter retirement.

At the time of writing, there are nevertheless a few apparently unstoppable survivors. Kim Il Sung of North Korea has been on the go for forty-five years. Kings Hussein of Jordan and Hassan of Morocco are well into their fourth decades. Elsewhere in Africa, Qaddafi, Houphouet-Boigny of the Ivory Coast, Hastings Banda of Malawi and Mobutu of the Congo believe they *are* the state. In a way they are correct, since most of their followers have known no other leader. As another long-term survivor, President Assad of Syria is said to have declared at the time of one attempted coup, 'You want to topple the regime? Here I stand, I am the regime.'

To demonstrate the case that leadership is largely about perception, one merely needs to watch what happens to the reputation of a leader when he or she resigns, retires or is defeated. Are their qualities, perceived earlier, retained? Or do they vanish the moment the seat of power is vacated? Compare Churchill and

Macmillan with Alec Douglas Home or Harold Wilson. Compare de Gaulle with almost any other postwar French politician. Where is Gerald Ford now? The perception of leadership, and the reputation for it, can be drastically short-lived. Ex-leaders are unwanted.

The desire to hold on to office come what may tempts some leaders into acts of greater and greater folly or even deviousness. Hence Richard Nixon and the Watergate conspiracy: this was the man who actually said, 'When the President does it, that means it's not illegal.' Having agreed to, or gone along with the illegal bugging of the Democratic headquarters and then having tried to cover the matter up, he resigned in 1974 just before being impeached.

The most dangerous moment for any country or organization is when good leaders retire, die or are deposed. If they have any choice in the matter they should not announce their departure a moment in advance, otherwise they immediately become lame ducks, with no future and therefore no present. A key function of any society should, consequently, be to ensure the smooth transfer of both leadership and administration. Nothing should be done before everyone is ready for the change. Thus the system keeps powerful men in the limelight as long as there is no chosen successor, even though ill-health or senility have set in, as with Churchill, Brezhnev and Chairman Mao. In some countries, like China, there has long been a tyranny of the old, with a slow process of leadership succession.

By contrast, Napoleon argued that the art of governing was not to allow men to grow old in their jobs. The Americans, along with many other countries, set a constitutional limit on the number of years or terms for which the nation's chief executive can hold office.

A sensible leader should aim at an efficient succession, if only because, if the organization collapses after his or her departure, history will blame them for not organizing things better. It is to be hoped, for example, that, after more than a decade in power, not only Mrs Thatcher's opponents and colleagues but also she herself will spend some more time considering what happens when she eventually steps down. Who is there who will be able to live up to her reputation, if not to her reality?

Megalomania, incidentally, is a latent danger with all long-term leaders. Lord Northcliffe was a great newspaper proprietor but increasingly he became intoxicated with his own power, in which the real was gradually eclipsed by the imaginary in his mind. Self-importance increases directly in relation to the length of time during which power is held. This is only natural. It is equally self-evident that measures should be taken to control it.

All democracies limit the length of terms for which governments hold office. When a term is over, the electors have a choice as to whether leaders deserve to be re-elected or ousted. The worth of the chief is subject to the judgement of the voter. A good leader will consequently hold his megalomania, his self-importance, in check, and balance out what he feels should be done with what he believes the electorate want in order to re-elect him. Oliver Cromwell's tenet, 'not what they want but what is good for them', carries little weight as the date of the election approaches.

There is a conflict in the greatest minds. Even moderately strong leaders want history to judge that none of their successors outshone them. The worst insult is to be forgotten, and some leaders' achievements disappear as soon as they do. Glory is fleeting, but obscurity is forever, as the saying goes. History is littered with war lords who created huge empires which disappeared virtually without trace when they did. The key is the extent to which a leader can control the choice of successor, or how much it is in the hands of fate, some board of directors, or a party junta.

Before I consider this further, let us consider the reasons why leaders fall from grace, other than ill health or mortality. Many of the qualities that make a good leader are curiously similar to those that may ensure their eventual downfall. Among these I would list:

1 A vivid independence.

2 Refusal to rely on others, leading to secretiveness or the attitude of, 'Don't question my decisions; I'm always right.'

3 A record of acting on gut feeling.

4 Single-mindedness, leading to tunnel vision.

5 Tough abrasiveness, leading to alienation of those around.

6 Speed of action.

7 Unpredictability and a mercurial nature.

We know the advantages of strong leadership. What are the drawbacks?

Firstly there is opposition to change. Strategies that have proved successful in the past are presumed to work for all time (and they may continue to be very efficiently managed, which is all the more dangerous). Secondly, potential successors are inhibited. How many strongly led companies in Britain and the U.S., are equally strongly led when the successor chairman comes along? As I have said earlier, good men below may for too long have been forced to quell any initiative or individual style, and may now be unable to throw off the habit.

The longer leaders occupy their positions, the more prone they are to abuse such qualities and thus turn them into failings. I find it hard to name a great leader who has appeared to be able to recognize latent personal weaknesses and neutralize them as required. Wounded emperors and injured presidents are sometimes the last to realize that in terms of their office they are terminally sick. And a demonstration of weakness in leadership does not last long. The last Tsar of the

Russias, Nicholas II, showed a lack of strength of purpose in contesting the Revolution, and abandoned by the aristocracy, who had been alienated by the conspiring of the Tsarina, he rapidly had to abdicate. Ex-leaders are bad news, a constant danger lurking in the wings. The Bolsheviks, like the French Revolutionaries in another age, wishing to ensure that the line would never return, assassinated the entire family at Ekaterinburg.

Neville Chamberlain is seen as one of the great failures of the twentieth century because of his policy of appeasement. While many shared his belief that the threat from Hitler was more perceived than real, his mistake was to dig himself ever deeper into the ditch of failure, apparently unable to recognize that he could be wrong. As Anthony Eden found later over Suez, the leader of an unpopular cause soon finds himself very alone.

Looking at it another way, the most common failings of leaders are:

1 A blindness to the need for change.

2 A belief in self that becomes *folie de grandeur*: the 'we have become a grandmother' syndrome.

3 Rigidity: the 'I've always done it this way and its worked' credo.

4 Not listening to impartial advisers, but choosing instead to listen to those sycophants who say what

they think you want to hear.

With reference to the last point, poor leaders, like poor managers, tend to encourage and promote their fans, real or apparent. Like-thinkers and, consequently, any ills in the system, are fostered and maintained. That is why constant challenge from without, from an effective opposition or from a threat such as an industrial takeover, can only be good for future efficiency by forcibly introducing new talent and a new culture to a moribund country or company.

It is a common political dictum that opposition parties don't win elections, but rather that incumbent leaders lose them. So it is in other walks of life as well. It is not generally for actions taken that leaders are thrown out, but for those *not taken* – over economic problems, drugs, crime and so on. This may be in spite of the fact that the leaders concerned are not actually to blame or even, in reality, able to control whatever the problems are. Because they are in the leadership seat they take the responsibility for failure, and they have to go. As the late Ian Macleod put it, with politicians the best time to kick them out is when they are on their way down. Scandal, personal weaknesses and arrogance also take their toll. Some great leaders ride all these things out for a while, as Macmillan and Thatcher did by *not* taking responsibility. When there was a cock-up, they shunned the blame and changed the management team instead. But in the end, they all go.

A final and not uncommon reason for the decline and fall of leaders is that power really does corrupt. Twice in the past I have seen, at first hand, corruption and the cult of personality taken to extremes of absurdity: once in Kwame Nkrumah's Ghana, and once in Nicolai Ceaucescu's Romania. It becomes laughable, but it is no laughing matter. Dictators don't set out to be dictators, but gradually, either because they get used to unquestioned power or in order to maintain their position, they take unconstitutional measures. They surround themselves with the weapons of suppression – secret police, *apparatchiks*, Tonton Macoute. They award themselves grand titles – Führer, Conducator (Ceaucescu) Osagefyo (Nkrumah the Redeemer) or Father of the Nation. Dictators such as Idi Amin of Uganda turn to brute force and terror at the expense of any economic or political sense. That force appears to be their strength but becomes instead their underlying weakness. When, in the mid-1970s, Amin expelled the Asian minority who ran most of Uganda's commerce, he effectively bankrupted the country and brought about his own downfall.

The Ceaucescu case is often misunderstood, which is understandable since until the Christmas revolution of 1989 few in the West knew anything about Romania, and the media carried little reporting since, by and large, Western journalists were refused entry. Ceaucescu was still remembered as the patriotic leader who was cheered by a million fellow citizens in Bucharest's main square when he condemned the Soviet invasion of Czechoslovakia in 1968. It had been a courageous thing to do. Romania too could have been occupied within a short day. But he survived, always the patriot and courted by the West, the man who would not let Warsaw Pact troops set foot on Romanian soil. Then, gradually, his absolute power corrupted him; his wife and family and a small coterie of flatterers, backed by the dreaded Securitate, gradually gathered unfettered and unchallenged power for more than two further decades.

When it came, the Romanian revolution was shown live on television. This was the struggle for power in the electronic age. For weeks after the overthrow of Ceaucescu, Studio 4 of the Romanian television station was the centre of the provisional government. Each broadcast became an act of the newly formed democracy. A dissident poet, Mircea Dinescu, appeared first, to shout, 'We've won, We've won.' The would-be leaders fought for position not in front of an electorate or a parliament but at the end of a television camera lens. Armed soldiers stood behind the announcers for days on end. Television was the embodiment of the revolution. It found the leaders. As such, it also became the goal of the counter-attacking Securitate as, again and again, they tried to storm the station. Staying on air meant staying free: as one commentator said, 'If television fails, the revolution fails.' It was an heroic image. It also made an interesting comparison with the long debate over when and how much to televise the British House of Commons.

There is hardly a great leader, sad to say, who is not a little devious at times in order to achieve his or her goals. This may only mean being economical with the truth, manipulating the media, stifling the preferment of able people, rewarding and awarding supporters and cronies and so on. But all too often it may lead on, as it did in President Nixon's case, to more devious or even criminal attempts, involving manipulation, perjury and who knows what else, to hold on to power.

In looking at the relationship between a dictator and the masses, it is strange to note, as Arnold Toynbee has commented, that human beings frequently acquiesce in, or even welcome or demand, dictatorships. The reason for this seems to be that it relieves all but the dictator of the agony of having to make crucial choices, particularly in crisis situations. Look at how Hitler's arrival was welcomed by much of Germany. A single leader in command of circumstances is reassuring. Autocracy is welcomed particularly by apathetic or anarchic societies who face external dangers. Once the danger has passed, then democratic government can once again be restored.

THE SUCCESSION

'In America, anyone can become President. Look at some of those who have.'

Variously attributed

A country, political party, company or even the local golf club must always have an eye on the succession stakes. But there are dangers. While, on the face of it, it is useful to have a crown prince waiting in the wings, things are seldom as tidy as that. Usually there are several crown princes or princesses, and they may well devote a lot of time and energy to squabbling over who is to sit on the throne. Either that or they are busy plotting to speed up the succession process by real or character assassination. Some simply mope in the corridors of power, waiting for dead men's shoes. Crown princes are, by definition, unsettling to have around. Good organizations and companies don't waste a lot of time appointing or encouraging them until they are really required. Good candidates for the top are left doing the jobs they do best.

Chosen crown princes are one thing. Self-elected ones are even more of a threat to an existing leader. They possess the necessary ambition to succeed. The result is often a vertical rather than a horizontal power struggle. Incumbent leaders try to circumvent this by finding out who their likely successors are and firing them. This doesn't always work: there are usually democratic constraints in any organization against such drastic action.

A leader faced with such circumstances may ensure continuing control by Balkanizing, or subdividing those under him into watertight compartments, setting prince against prince. Thus only the leader knows what this minister or that governor is up to. This system is often highly impracticable in reality, but most chiefs try it on notwithstanding, in an attempt to retain some control over their likely successor and to prevent those below ganging up to do the unseating.

British colonialists used the divide and rule technique throughout the empire. If one chief got too big or aggressive it was delicately suggested that he was more of a threat to other chiefs than to the British governor. Geographical boundaries were carefully drawn to support this policy. To take a different example, robber barons seldom conquered their anarchical leanings and their own self-interests in order to unite against the king. Where their modern counterparts start to do so, in cabinet or boardroom, a clever leader can usually appeal to the selfish ambitions of the would-be conspirators with the question, 'O.K. so you want to unseat me, but which of you is going to take my chair? Why don't I sit back and watch you fight over it first?'

On the way up any ladder in any organization, the key to getting to the top depends on whether someone is already on the step above. If there is only one leadership position and that is already filled, then no one else can fill it as well. The incumbent first has to go, by coup, by resignation, by promotion to some other function, or by falling to the Great Reaper – or the contender must fail. Other candidates for the post, whatever the Balkan fiefdom they have been confined to, have, equally, to be disposed of on the way to the throne.

In some hierarchies the Peter Principle still holds true. (Dr Peter argued that if you are competent at one level of responsibility you tend to be promoted until you go beyond your ability. As a corollary, you thus have the greatest power when you are least capable of wielding it.) Increasingly, in the new competitive age, such inadequacy is less tolerated. Systems don't promote incompetents.

This leads, alternatively, to the *Shea theorem: Good organizations are good at moving incompetent people to positions where their incompetence does not matter.* This means moving them sideways, out, or, in politics, to a contented retirement on the back benches complete with knighthood, or to the House of Lords.

However, my antitheorem states: *Many good organizations are bad at getting rid of incompetents usually for (wrong) 'humanitarian' reasons.* It may be easier to attain a leadership position than to maintain it. Getting there may require only temporary flair. As many selection boards know to their cost, someone who interviews well may not, ultimately, be able to sustain the promise. Holding on requires perseverance, consistency, courage and ego.

The final skill is knowing when and how to hand over the reins.

Conclusions

'Men are of no importance. What counts is who commands them.'

Napoleon

THE NATURE OF LEADERSHIP

1 Never confuse leadership with the apparent status of the position held. Many so-called leaders are mere marionettes, bubble figures who have floated to the surface by not putting feet wrong and creating fewest enemies.

2 Big bureaucracies can carry marionettes. Small units cannot.

3 Marionettes and the weak organizations below them need to be dressed up by the image-makers of life. The latter are skilled at cloaking inaction and inefficiency.

4 Leaders and managers are very different animals. Managers, like administrators, are interested in working within given parameters. Their vision is limited within a set framework. Leaders don't ack-

nowledge parameters: they create new landscapes and new horizons.

5 Leaders are seldom perceived to be good, bad or indifferent until they have held office for some time. A verdict of history, no matter how short, is required. But they may bring a reputation with them from subordinate posts, and that may take time to change.

6 Leadership requires certain management skills, but is not limited by them. It is created by inherited and environmental factors.

7 Intelligence does not necessarily endow qualities of leadership.

8 Leadership is not a science but an art.

9 Some leadership skills can be acquired; other dormant skills can be brought to the surface by clever training programmes.

10 Leadership is frequently acquired by chance; by the seizing of opportunities presented, at the right time, by the right person.

11 A manager can make a good team work well. A good manager can make an average team work well. A true leader can change the whole attitude, philosophy and spirit of any group of people.

12 A real leader's confidence will inspire confidence in others.

13 Leaders from all walks of life share some common leadership characteristics. They move easily from one leadership slot to another.

14 In conclusion, leaders rule by realizing the following twenty keys to success.

THE RULES OF LEADERSHIP

1 It is easier to get there than to stay there.

2 There are no office hours. It's a one-hundred-and-sixty-eight hour week.

3 When conducting the orchestra never turn your back on the audience.

4 If you forget how you got there, you won't stay long.

5 You have to set goals, then beat them.

6 You have to set your followers the same goals.

7 You have to keep a bright, young staff to keep yourself up to the mark and thinking fresh. At the same time you should not ignore the wisdom of the mature.

8 Sometimes you have to divide in order to rule.

9 You need to inspire deputies with some artificially inspired, creative tension.

10 Old and proven strategies must constantly be

looked at in new ways.

11 The team has to be kept active on new strategies and goals as a tactic for constant fresh thinking.

12 You have to persist, persist and persist again.

13 You must take a lead, but listen and respond.

14 You have to prevent unwise decisions before taking wise ones. Watch for the banana skin, it's always there.

15 Remind yourself that leadership is about causes and is not an end in itself.

16 Motivate and reward enthusiasm, drive and success.

17 Be accessible and visible to those who are strategically and personally important. Maintain a distance: it lends mystique.

18 Keep working on your communication skills. You don't have to be liked, but your policies and results do.

19 Learn to delegate and motivate; organize and chastise; praise and raise.

20 Image and perception outlast reality.

These are the leadership rules in any walk of life.

Index